Slices of Life

Slices of Life

Perspectives on a Woman's World

Linda Andersen

BAKER BOOK HOUSE
Grand Rapids, Michigan 49506

Copyright 1986 by
Baker Book House Company

ISBN: 0-8010-0205-2

Printed in the United States of America

Scripture references are taken from the Holy Bible: New International
Version copyright © 1973, 1978, 1984 by the International Bible Society.
Used by permission of Zondervan Bible Publishers.

"Is Every Morning Monday?" was originally printed in *Today's Christian
Woman*. Some other chapters were originally printed in the Woman's
World column of *Discovery Digest,* a copyright publication of the Radio
Bible Class. Used with permission.

To
His Majesty,
King Jesus

Contents

Preface

This book is not the result of having climbed up in
some imaginary tower and emerged with a portfolio of
salable stories. Rather, it's like a hallway of picture windows looking deeply into the human experience of each
of us. Each "window" is a look at a slice of life and each
has a distinct view all its own. The incidents were lived
day by day and sometimes tear by tear. Most of them
occurred in a year's time and were written while the les-
sons were still fresh and some of the crises unresolved.

To share experiences such as these is to take them out
of storage, dust them off, and offer them to God to
polish and redeem. This he has done and is continuing
to do. I don't share merely to stir emotions but to point
always to the Jesus who is the redeemer not only of the
eternal soul, but also of desert experiences. I want to
introduce you to a faithful friend who walks with us
even when we can't see his footprints or hear his voice.

This book is for you to enjoy and pass on to those

9

who want *their* experiences redeemed, their timid faith recharged. The experiences are a joyous affirmation that our mighty God, Prince of Peace, is still in the business of redeeming the otherwise unredeemable.

A Meditation

I gave him nothing he really needed when I gave him all I had. And in return he gave me all I would ever need—and more.

The exchange was unequal—myself and my poverty for an eternity of fellowship and riches and inner prosperity. In an invisible moment emblazoned on time, eternal life and forgiveness were gifted to me, and eternal death and guilt were forever taken away. A shaft of song and light pierced deep inside the cleansed cavern of my being and sent up anthems that would never fade. Love notes rose like crashing cymbals, and my salvation song would be part of me forever.

It was loud and clear, this song of mine, and melodic. I soon found others who knew the same song, and we sang it joyfully together.

Years flew by and the song remained: now muted, now bold and strong. Sometimes I couldn't read the notes for the tears, but that happened only when I took my eyes off the Conductor.

Often the song surged and swelled in a joyous tumble of praise and hallelujahs. And the meaning was born anew each morning.

> *The LORD is my strength and my song;*
>   *he has become my salvation.*
> *He is my God, and I will praise him;*
>   *my father's God, and I will exalt him.* [Exod. 15:2]

Today Is Mine

Creation. It's only 7:30, and already my family has scattered in four directions. How very American! I sit on the steps and drink in great drafts of morning poured out of a sun-filled sky, and I am content. Through my screen door filters the aroma of perking coffee, and a cloud of swallows plays hide-and-seek around the barn. So early, yet I already have small pocketfuls of life to take the sharp edges off the rest of today. My mind floats back to the beginning, when God said, "Let there be light," and there was light! Day 1 leaped into existence! My heart overflows with gratitude to the Creator of the very first day—and of this day.

People. Today my husband kissed me, while I was still eating. It takes a lot of character to do that!

Today I got waves and smiles from neighbor kids at the bus stop. They were genuine, happy smiles—the kind that make me smile on the inside.

Senses. Today I sit here in perfectly sound health and

13

watch the morning sun lay strips of gold sequins across an emerald sea of grass. I watch a family of yellow butterflies swarm in dizzying circles above the spirea bush. Today I smell the flowers and hear the simmering sounds of midsummer and feel a silken breeze as it strokes the giant maples. In the beginning, when God created all this beauty, he looked at each splendid segment and said it was good. And it still is!

Memories. Today I remember some yesterdays. So many of them were good. The first smile of each baby shone like a sunrise. First steps echoed with happiness. They walked all the way across my heart and left tiny footprints that would never fade. First words were giants of joy. First sentences caused celebrations. Little hands and big smiles, lunchpails and pigtails, crayons and graham crackers; all live in yesterday's pocket of memories. But that was yesterday.

Today. Today is a hallway of a hundred unopened doors. And God has the key to all of them. He's had the key for a long time. I've told him he can come and go without knocking because he purchased this property. He belongs here—in today—in tomorrow. I hug my armload of blessings and feel thankfulness sweep away fear and worry.

The coffee is done. Today stands at attention. My work awaits. I wonder what else is waiting? Maybe tragedy, or tears, or grinding pain. I have no guarantees, except the only one I need: God will walk with me through every door I enter today. And today, as always, that is enough. As for yesterday, I let it go. As for tomorrow, it may not come. Today, and only today, is my gift to unwrap and enjoy.

Glory in the Morning

It's 5:30 A.M., and Day knocks at the dark doors of Night. I sit on my porch swing under a dark-green umbrella of maple leaves that hover maternally over the porch roof. And I wait for Sun.

A thin wisp of steam hovers expectantly over the coffee cup I hold. The air vibrates with ecstatic birdsong. "Cat" curls beside me for her final nap before breakfast. Morning-glories prepare to unfurl blue trumpets. Then it happens, and I am as awestruck as if I had never seen a sunrise.

Curtains of Night draw back silently, and Sun bursts merrily over the blue haze of distant hills, painting earth in green and brown stripes. It is morning . . . and it is glorious!

I listen, and hear Sun whistle a song of new opportunity. I hear Nature's first day-song waiting to be sung, and am reminded that "this *is* the day the Lord has made." And I decide to "rejoice and be glad in it."

I can almost hear the boisterous "hello!" of newly-awakened Nature saying, "Aw, c'mon. Time's a-wastin'." I sense the warm "Good morning, child" of a loving heavenly Father who has promised his children he will never leave or forsake them, and who can't break his word.

Concerns of the day start pushing in, and I push back, giving the gift of sunrise a chance to pour full energy and a healthy share of humor into this new section of time carved out for me by the almighty Daygiver.

All is not perfectly well on earth. No matter. I will set my face toward *the* Son and fix my desires on the promises of God for this day. I will decide not to doubt now what I took for granted in better times: his love and care.

Who, after all, causes Sun to rise? And who causes it to set? And if he could take care of that since the beginning of time, can't I also assume—no, believe—that he can also make arrangements for my life? Without question, I can.

Sunrise . . . the tie that binds man to earth and earth to heaven. The faithful reminder that God cares for his creatures.

From his perch on the great maple, a bird cocks his head, opens a tiny beak, and spills out a spirited song of morning celebration—of sunrise—of a new day and fresh strength and endless possibilities. I pick up my cup, now grown cool, and begin my day with joy.

Thoughts on God's Country

The country and I have a real "thing" going. It's as simple and as profound as that. I love it. The country is a forever friend and my favorite part of God's creative energies.

As a listener, the country has no peer. Take corn stalks, for instance. They never talk back. They don't give unasked-for advice. They simply listen. Pine woods don't challenge or scold either. They listen and whisper sweet nothings back to me. Wildflowers don't demand my time and attention. They just do what they do best—look pretty. It seems to me that the countryside is all give and no take.

Spring

A country springtime gives me new life as it shakes off the cumbersome shackles of Old Man Winter and kicks its way to resurrection after resurrection. A crocus:

stubbornness dressed in lavender; energetic, pushing up even through crusted snow. Daffodils: yellow and laughing. A rose: classic perfection. Spring is an all-time favorite of mine, and a season I'm hoping will be in heaven all year 'round.

Summer

In Michigan, summer in the country is a new way of life. People and animals come out of hibernation. I don't need the calendar to tell me when summer has arrived. The tractors tell me. The smell of fresh chicken manure being plowed into the ground tells me. The robins shout it every morning and sunshine is a regular customer. Ah, summer. I throw my head back and drink in the sounds of people and dogs and tractors and children and bicycles and birds. Dim winter eyes feast on the sights and sounds of full, hot summer days in the country, and wish them to stay forever.

Fall

I'm spurred to action with the first chill breeze of fall. It's time to settle in for the winter—time to haul dry wood to the porch for cold winter blasts to come—time to gather grapes and can purple juice to drink on black winter nights—time to wash storm windows and try to put them up before the first snowstorm—time to walk through our leaf-carpeted patchwork of woods for one last time—time to lay up food stores from the garden and transform a tomato on the vine into a jar of sparkling red juice—time to winterize the car and rake and burn the leaves—time to batten down the hatches before the hurricane of winter knocks at the door.

Winter

Winter, white and cold, gives me time to reflect, to read, and read some more. Winter is a quiet, kindly pause between fall and spring, and good for rocking beside wood stoves and stoking up fireplaces. Winter, silent and still, is a friend when I cross-country ski and lose pounds in the process. Winter is a chance to allow God to strengthen body and soul alike as I battle the season in a thousand different ways—as I shovel snow, scrape ice, thaw pipes, and carry in groceries during blizzards. Winter, for me, is a test. It asks each year in November, "Can you make it through this year?" Toward the end of March, I always wonder, but then comes spring right smack in the middle of March, shouting, "I'm here! Just like always, I'm here."

People

The people of the country are real—without sham and veneer—stripped down to the essentials of love and warmth and compassion. Country people are authentic. Their blood beats in deep, red rivers through strong bodies, and stalwart souls seem somehow to trust God easier than some I've met. I have met country people in different states, different settings. They are essentially the same. Frank. Open. Real. Next to God.

Earth

Is it any wonder that the country and I have fallen in love? I think not. The country is closer to God somehow. I close my eyes on a fall day in the piney woods, and I know it. My eyes sweep the calico landscape of harvest-time, and I know it. I watch the corn change from seed-ling to six-foot stalk, and I know it. I eat a tomato that began with a seed, and I know it. I watch cherry trees burst into a white froth of foaming blossoms and I can't challenge it. God *must* love the country better—he seems to spend so much time there.

The country and I were meant for each other. Cement jungles have no allure for me. The tinsel towns of the world are just that—shallow imitations of the "real stuff" one finds outside the city limits and a "fur piece" into the best of all worlds—God's country.

Oatmeal Days

It's not always the red–flag crisis days that are hardest to take. It's the "oatmeal days." The ordinary, "zero" days of little or no consequence. The ho–hum days filled with nothing of any particular interest. Colorless. Uninteresting. Unfascinating. Unspectacular. And unfun. The days everyone deals with. The hours of private frustration and closeted tears. The times of nagging pain. The lonesome times of spiritual desert. The prolonged times of chronic illness no one really wants to hear about. The days when it seems as if God isn't there.

Cheery cards seldom come to lighten the load when things are ordinary. Few if any concerned callers wrap layers of warmth around us. There are no visits from friends bearing gifts of food or entire meals. No offers of housecleaning. No baking. No baby-sitting. Nothing. We cope. We wend our way through the tangle of tedious activity and sandpaper people scattered through our day and get no applause, because coping is expected.

21

Not so during the red-flag crisis times. Events may be cruelly ripped from our control, but in his own special God-way, our Father seems to walk especially close, to be especially real. People tend to rally behind us with loving support. We are lifted above the crisis and enabled beyond human comprehension at times. And *we* get applause, because people tend to forget that it's our God at work. The prayers of scores of friends reach the Father and make a resounding difference—*until the crisis is over,* until people return to oatmeal days of their own, and leave you with the God who is more than enough anyway.

On oatmeal days, after a crisis has peaked, it may seem as if friends have forsaken us, as if God doesn't care. But the reality will be that life has merely pushed us and our friends one step further in the Christian growth-walk. This Father-God of ours is waiting in the wings of heaven, making sense out of tangled human experiences every day, just as he promised (Rom. 8:28). It's time to move forward softly, where God is waiting to take us by the hand, and light the way, and clear away the underbrush.

The God of the crisis times is the God of the oatmeal days too. Because he said he is. Because he keeps his promises—always. Because we can't get along without him. And because we wouldn't want to if we could.

The Great Cleanup

In the private dugout of my thoughts, I remembered the week just ended . . . a week of hand-picked days set aside to clean my house like it had *never* been cleaned . . . to reestablish order. It was the culmination of reshuffled dental appointments and shopping trips and company. The days were mine alone.

I began on the east side of the house and moved westward, wielding dustcloth in one hand and mop in the other. Monday tossed her first-of-the-week sunbeams into every cobwebbed corner, and a song chased through my head. From eight o'clock in the morning until four o'clock in the afternoon, I was a bulldozer in tennis shoes, moving relentlessly from ceiling to walls, to floors to curtains to bedding. I spread sparkle and shine in a path behind me. Two rooms a day . . . I was on schedule. On to my son's room. One whole day there! Then the attic became respectable. And we could see through the windows again! Maybe I *didn't* need glasses. Just me and my radio and a mind free to create, plan, decide, and pray. "Thanks, Lord, and watch out, family, here I come!"

Thursday. Unexpected company. Still on schedule. Moving right along. Friday. Company leaves early. Almost there! Puffing again. Wearing down. Feeling good inside. Coffee break . . . a-h-h-h. Why is Kelly frowning? She had those magazines for five years.

"Your timing is so good," I told my unexpected company. "My house has never been so clean." Every inch of me smiled.

Her reply came softly, stood on tiptoe, and shouted through my pride: "But I don't care how clean your house is, Linda." Her unspoken words said, "I care about you." And she did. She cared about the people inside.

I remembered stumbling rudely over the feelings and preferences of "the people inside" this week in my rush to establish order. I looked several years into the future and knew which they would remember. I cast a prayer straight through my shining ceiling. "Lord!" It was hard to go on. "I did it again!" He had been waiting for that. He always waits as long as it takes. And he communed softly with my need and wiped away the shadow and poured fresh pitchers of living water.

It didn't seem that bad. It wasn't *that* noticeable. Or was it? It wasn't robbery . . . or murder . . . or child abuse. But if it had been, God's response would have been the same. Forgiveness, restoration, and joy. And that's what brought the tears.

If we confess our sins, he is faithful and just and will forgive us our sins and purify us from all unrighteousness. [1 John 1:9]

Fledgling

"Don't worry," cries Dark-Eyes as she prepares to leave the nest. "Don't worry." And she rushes uninitiated into the waiting arms of a world she hasn't met.

Confidently, tossing her curls, she walks head-on into the arena I know too well. The world of fleeting joys, bright allure, and frequent disappointment . . . plastic, shining promises and dark surprises and elusive happiness.

But I'm a mother, and a mother has the right to worry! It's her prerogative! Mothers were born to say, "Tie your hood" (Don't get a cold, I hate to see you suffer), "Put on your life jacket" (Please stay alive . . . I love you), and "Don't forget to pray" (Don't forget God).

And as the child grows older words change color but mean the same: "Share the bathroom" (Don't become selfish); "Come home early" (Temptations abound out there); "Is he a Christian?" (I don't want your life to be miserable). They are all familiar mother-ways of saying, "I love you."

But Dark-Eyes and other fledglings don't always understand when they're busy flapping their wings at the edge of the nest. And they don't like orders . . . from anyone.

Sometimes they try their wings, leave the nest, and don't tell you when they are coming home. And the lump in your throat and the sleepless night speak softly into the darkness, saying, "I love you. Don't get hurt. Be careful."

But maybe "worry" isn't the right word—at least not the word that *has* to be. I stand in the nest I've lined so carefully and comfortably, watching Dark-Eyes make plans with purpose and daring, yet without the whole armor of God . . . without the ability to stand against the wiles of the enemy of her soul (Eph. 6:11), without the helmet of salvation, the sword of the Spirit, the breastplate of righteousness, and the shield of faith. I climb daily . . . hourly into the arms of a heavenly Father who reminds me plainly not to be overly anxious about anything (Phil. 4:6). I ask him if it isn't more spiritual to be "concerned," and he says no. I ask him if it won't help, and he says no (Matt. 6:27). He goes on further, in his Word, ordering me not to worry and explaining that he is in charge.

Then I understand. If I plunge ahead into a sea of worry about Fledgling or anything else, I am a disobedient child myself! I am breaking the faith—ignoring the rules. I am mutinous. I dare not disobey, or I'll pay in sleeplessness, missed joys, and lack of spiritual growth. His order to me is just as firm as his orders for her. And I'm taken aback when I realize it is just as important for me to obey as it is for her.

Fledgling's life is her own. I can't live it for her. And that's okay. Because I must let God be God here, too. I read the order again: "Do not be anxious about anything, but in everything, by prayer and petition, with thanksgiving, present your requests to God. And the peace of God, which transcends all understanding, will guard your hearts and your minds in Christ Jesus" (Phil. 4:6–7).

I look up, and *really* see the stubborn joy of a green-gold spring morning all laden with birdsong and cherry blossoms waving happy white flags against blue sky. And Dark-Eyes waves good-by.

History has repeated itself. I recall my mother, myself as a fledgling, and I walk out into a day full of smiling possibilities . . . because he lives!

No Way Out?

A young girl stepped up to the large, brightly lit counter and placed her order in brisk tones: "Satisfaction, please. Enough to last a lifetime."

The sign over the counter read:

WORLD SYSTEMS, INC.
PLACE YOUR ORDER HERE

A uniformed man began stacking colorful boxes on the counter. She read the labels with interest: Sex. Love. Fame. Money. Friends. Music. Alcohol. Drugs. And there were more.

"There." The clerk's cheery voice startled her. "That ought to do it. Sign here, please, and the boxes are yours." With a stroke of the pen she signed her life over to World Systems and walked away, smiling. Her friends had sampled the contents of most of these boxes, and she could hardly wait to join them in her quest for satisfaction.

She opened Sex first, and soon she lost her innocence and sense of personal worth to a married man. An unexpected pregnancy led her to have an abortion, which left her womanly senses bruised and aching for the life she had taken.

Next came Love. That brought her satisfaction—until he decided he was in too deep and skipped town without letting her know.

Fame sounded wonderful, too. She scratched and clawed, working to make her name a byword in every American home. She wanted to be the American idol. But at home . . . in the dark . . . when she was all alone . . . the hollowness inside her made perspiration break out on her forehead and caused her hands to tremble.

Money was the twin of Fame, and she somehow felt that when she had enough money, satisfaction would follow. But how much was enough?

She opened the Friends box, and she did find much satisfaction in friends. Until her best friend got killed. Until one by one the others drifted away for one reason or another. Until they had left her alone on her self-made island.

Music was an interesting box. She tried the theme songs of the World Systems, Incorporated, and found that they spoke her language. They were sad, hopeless, angry, rebellious songs. They fed her soul day and night. They formed her thoughts and molded her actions. Satisfaction? Not exactly. And what satisfaction there was disappeared the moment the music stopped.

The next box was Alcohol. Surely this would take the bitter edge off her consciousness. Surely it would disguise the obvious lack of satisfaction in her life. She drank deeply. And when she looked in the mirror, she was shocked to discover that alcohol had robbed her of her youth and vigor and put a look of hopelessness in her eyes.

Drugs were a last resort. If satisfaction was not to be found here, then where? But drugs also deceived her. Just when she thought they had given her peace, she awoke to find herself in a pitiful, personal, screaming hell. There was no way out . . . there was no way back . . . unless . . .

She was growing older. There wasn't much time. She remembered some words she had heard over and over again as a child. She had rejected them vehemently then. "I am the way and the truth and the life. No one comes to the Father except through me . . . Whoever comes to me I will never drive away . . . Streams of living water will flow from within him . . . Come to me, all you who are weary and burdened, and I will give you rest." The Bible verses flowed together as she cast back and forth for a solution.

Then, in a sudden decisive move she packaged the contents of every box and returned them to World Systems. She didn't ask for a refund. She placed them on the counter, turned her back on them, and walked away— never to look back. Confessing her abject poverty of spirit, she saw Jesus only. He had been there all the time, waiting patiently in line. He welcomed her back into the arms of his forgiving, caring love.

I thought in my heart, "Come now, I will test you with pleasure to find out what is good." But that also proved to be meaningless. "Laughter," I said, "is foolish. And what does pleasure accomplish?" I tried cheering myself with wine, and embracing folly—my mind still guiding me with wisdom. I wanted to see what was worthwhile for men to do under heaven during the few days of their lives. [Eccles. 2:1–3]

Your enemy the devil prowls around like a roaring lion looking for someone to devour. [1 Peter 5:8]

"Whoever finds his life will lose it, and whoever loses his life for my sake will find it." [Matt. 10:39]

For a man's ways are in full view of the LORD. . . . [Prov. 5:21]

"I am the bread of life. He who comes to me will never go hungry, and he who believes in me will never be thirsty." [John 6:35]

"For God so loved the world that he gave his one and only Son, that whoever believes in him shall not perish but have eternal life." [John 3:16]

" 'Rejoice with me; I have found my lost sheep.' I tell you that in the same way there will be more rejoicing in heaven over one sinner who repents than over ninety-nine righteous persons who do not need to repent." [Luke 15:6–7]

Windows

White-bibbed mountaintops and orderly rows of artichokes spin past our train windows in a green-brown blur. She is fifteen years old; I am forty-three.

The double seats are filled, so we sit separately on either side of the aisle. My window is on the left, hers on the right. Mine overlooks little houses and sun-bronzed people and railroad tracks. Hers frames massive mountain peaks ornamented with blue-gray cloud masses and streaks of glittering sun.

At first I try to get her to watch scenes from my window. Faint frown lines form on her teen-age brow, so I decide to enjoy my view and let her enjoy hers.

I steal a sidelong glance at her clean profile. I know she sees different scenery than I. She is she and I am I. God has seen to that. He has created us with different antennae. Why, then, do I so often insist that she enjoy the scenery from my "windows" and in my way? I think it over.

We will have two different stories to tell. Will one be true and one untrue? Will one be the "best" view or the "right" view? Not necessarily. The same ride will be described from two different perspectives and sets of perceptions. Isn't it that way a lot? With others too? Don't we each walk into similar experiences wearing different glasses . . . reacting in different ways? And isn't it all too easy to condemn that very differentness as wrongness? Do my daughter or others have to always see life from my "windows"? It is too easy to forget that God is in the ongoing process of forming that beloved (or unbeloved) "other" in his own way and in his own time. It is easy to stumble over the rainbow of creative difference in others in the rush to insist they look out our "windows."

But perhaps it is the hardest with children. Bone of my bone and flesh of my flesh. But their windows are different from mine. Their God-given perceptions—their windows—deserve respect and consideration.

I cut the umbilical cord—again—and wish my daughter freedom from future "others" who would clone her if they could. A fragment of Scripture plays in my mind: "Train up a child in the way *he* should go" . . . prayerful, guided freedom to develop unhampered before God . . . to fulfill her created purposes . . . to see clearly through *her* windows.

Of Seasons and Children

Spring

Elusive Springchild: You're a runaway sunbeam, touching us all with your original birdsong. Advance guard of summer, that's what you are, making your quiet, shy entrance on the icy heels of winter, and melting the ice of our private frozen landscapes.

Springchild: always fresh, always new, always welcome with your winsome, charming smile. The lazy, yawning yearning of nature, conceived in winter's chilling womb and born anew each season. You radiate the fragrant spirit of a willingness to wait—to bide your time—to be born in the right moment.

Springchild: the standing ovation of winter. We've been waiting for you. How quickly we take you to our hearts. Draped in the muted yellows and pinks of Easter, you make your debut with joyful song, plucking delicately at rusty heartstrings. Go ahead. Plant your seeds of joy and watch green shoots push their way through crusted clay lives grown brittle.

Earth needs you, Springchild, to soften, to heal, to find harmony once again in the many faces of tragedy. Go ahead and bloom! Glisten! Glow! It's in your nature. Pale blush of early spring, you paint our gray horizons with liquid gold and prop a pillow behind every hard place.

Father, take this tender shoot of mine. Protect the sensitivity and guard the gentleness. Use the ever-present birdsong to brighten a world that is insensitive to beauty and joy, and to your love.

Summer

Summerchild: Lush, green Summerchild, that's you! Alive and humming with madcap activity. Always making waves and riding them all the way to shore.

Noisy, affectionate, steamy Summerchild. Arms warm and receptive, small enough for one person but wide enough for the whole world. Certainly strong enough to tie knots in everyone's emotions. Brandishing sunshine like a sword, you ride into lives with glowing ardor in your gamy, spicy ways—seasoned with laughter and a dash of pepper. Hot-air artist that you are, you bring deep summer with all its pageantry and flash to the world. Your pendulum swings from sultry and torpid to turbulent. Bright smile, flashing grin. We're awash in the warmth of your summer colors, summer fragrance.

Summerchild: Always melting the ice on our mountains, exhausting us with activity, delighting us with your tropical plumage and frightening us with your summer squalls. You are bright, bubbly prisms of sunshine

35

in unexpected places. You are shocking but honest. You are shifting moods and bright surprises. You are inspiration with the new notes in your birdsong since Christ became your personal friend. A season all to yourself, Summerchild, and all for the world.

Father, tone down the noise but don't drown the song. Calm the turbulence, but don't extinguish the lightning. Use the summer of my children to prod the languishing souls who have lost heart, and give them reasons to laugh again just because they're alive—and because you are alive.

Autumn

Autumnchild: You're summer with an overcoat on; the express beauty of all the seasons bound up in one, final, ceremonial flourish of color. Autumnchild: back door of summer and front door of winter.

You tiptoe out of summer cautiously poised, almost somber. You take cool command of your season and appear unruffled by what's ahead. Your entrance into the outer courtyard of winter is quietly proud, regal, self-possessed. Suddenly there is color—then the summer leaves are no more.

You march steadily toward winter, cooling our fevered activity and moderating the frantic pace of our harvesttimes. Yours is a measured step, in tune with the yawn of nature as she prepares for her seasonal nap.

Autumnchild that you are, you waver with seasonal indecision: first warm, then cool, then standing still, poised in an Indian-summer stance. You slide naturally between summer and winter—a buffer zone of quiet, predictable pleasure. You are autumn, and you are a distinctive celebration of color and sight and sound.

Father, warm the heart that would too easily become iced over. Stir the coals and ignite a flame that wll start him in the right direction. Pierce the armor of self-reliance with just enough poverty to keep pride at bay. And remind Autumnchild that you created him for a reason.

Winter

Winterchild: You're the king of all seasons. You flex your giant muscles all cloaked in ice and dare us to challenge your power. Confident in strength, you bluster and storm about with gale-force winds to get your way. You often leave a blizzard in your wake.

Big brother of fall, you stand head and shoulders above all seasons. Winterchild, your strength is overwhelming, indomitable. You're brimming with striking possibilities . . . for good and for bad. You are gale winds and arctic blasts. But you are also tranquil snowflakes and the calming hush of winter sunsets. You're strong but gentle, mighty but moldable, a giant with a tear in his eye. Your roar is deceptive, your tenderness unexpected. Stand strong in your possibilities, Winterchild, for they are awesome.

Father, temper the steel in this, your Winterchild. Make him strong enough to carry a heavy load because he may have to. Make him flexible enough to be human because he may need to be. And help him in times of personal weakness not to bluster louder, but to pray more.

—A Mother

A Home Is a Home Is a Home

I continued my reading in Edith Schaeffer's *What Is a Family*: "A home is meant to reflect the interests, tastes, abilities of those living there, and *not* to reflect the showroom window of the furniture store."

I looked over at Kelly's softball mitt plopped unceremoniously on the buffet beside my picture-perfect dried flowers. Schoolbooks were stacked pell-mell to the right. "So far, so good," I said to no one in particular.

I saw the towels draped over kitchen-chair backs to dry (my husband's idea of saving money). I drifted to the boot porch and eyed five pairs of tennis shoes (for all occasions), four pairs of muddied work boots (for husband and son), three pairs of worn-out gardening shoes (why three?), and the ever-present shower clogs (better known as flip-flops).

A glance at the spare room showed sewing-machine clutter (that's me) and stacks of folded but unclaimed laundry (that's them). Uh-huh. That's us. Edith, you'd be proud.

On the stairs, I tripped over a candleholder (mine from three weeks ago) and a stack of Bibles (from Sunday). Kelly's unmade bed was covered with freshly-cut pictures of the Tigers baseball team. The Tigers came before anything these days.

Dean's room was a delight to the woman who wants her home to fully reflect family activities and interests (I wasn't too sure I did). The dresser was mounded with everything from muscle-building equipment to three-year-old undeveloped film.

I read on. "Sometimes, an unvacuumed floor is 'healthy air' when you need a break from routine." I glanced at mine and headed for the hammock. "Sometimes," the book went on, "people need a special place to build, to mold, to be themselves." Dawn's room qualified. Her walls were covered with signatures of her friends. And dust balls held daily reunions under her bed.

"Creativity is stifled by a too-rigid routine," Schaeffer wrote. A plus for our disappearing mealtimes? My neatly circumscribed six o'clock dinners had gotten lost between softball and cheerleading.

Did God fit into all of this too? I had to believe he did, because I am his workmanship, placed in his arena along with four other growing Christians. I looked around, and purposely believed God was at work—because he was.

Verna's Secret

She lives alone in tiny, second-story rooms above a weatherbeaten general store and gas station that have seen better days. No one has used them for years. Verna Bok has been a widow for forty years, I learned one Sunday after church. This diminutive lady without a car is always in church (when she's well), and she's always smiling. I wondered why as I watched her come and go, leaning heavily on her cane.

The blinds at Verna's windows are slightly askew, and the building she lives in looks perpetually deserted and forgotten. A lone gas pump sits stolidly out in front near the road like a paunchy, middle-aged man with nothing much to do except watch the traffic go by. The old, sun-faded pump hasn't served our lazy little community in more years than anyone can remember. The cost of gasoline still reads thirty-one cents a gallon—just as if inflation never happened—just as if it remembers a time when our tiny farming town boasted enough "live" businesses to keep the main road buzzing with activity. Verna remembers those days well enough. Now business has gone elsewhere, leaving the village of Forest Grove and Verna to grow old together. But Verna Bok is not a person who merely sits still and grows old, as I soon discovered.

I was having some neighbors in one evening, and on a sudden impulse I decided to include Verna.

"How nice!" she beamed over the telephone wire connecting our voices. "How very nice of you to call. I'd surely come if only I was well enough." She had been sick for a couple of weeks up there alone in that tiny apartment. I was sorry, and I told her so.

"You must get awfully lonesome, Verna."

"Lonesome?" She sounded surprised. "Oh my, no," she bubbled, laughing. "Why, I'm never lonesome." (I had a feeling I was about to discover something.) "You see, I have all my good memories to keep me company—and my photograph albums too. And then, 'a course, I keep so busy with Ruth's boys."

"Oh?" I asked, before remembering that she had a nearby neighbor named Ruth.

"Oh yes," she replied. "You see, Ruth has eight boys, and she works, ya know. So's I fix supper for them boys every night. Yes, I been doin' it for years now. It saves her a whole lot of worry, and it gives me sumthin' useful to do. Oh, yes, them boys gets me flowers too, on Mother's Day. They're like m' own boys." Now I knew that this was an unusual person indeed. And I began to understand the secret of her youthful exuberance for life.

Verna had learned something that most people take a lifetime to discover, and she had found it less than a country mile from her own home. Without actually looking for happiness, she had kept herself busy filling the empty cups of other people's lives.

When my husband greeted Verna in church one morning some weeks later, he commented on the stunning pair of cardinals he had spotted in our maple trees. "Verna," he emphasized, "they would have knocked your eyes out!" Her warm eyes brightened, and her familiar smile appeared.

"Oh, yes," she chuckled. "And you know, I heard the most beautiful wren song just this morning." She shook her finger for emphasis as she talked. "I get up early every day, ya know, so's I don't miss a thing. I like to watch the houses around here wake up, don'tcha know. Yessir, there's so much ta see—so much ta see. And I enjoy everything God made—everything, don'tcha see?" The secret was finally out.

Verna, you get up to see what most of us miss, or ignore, or are just too busy to enjoy. You magnify the pluses God places all over your small world. You seem to paint a rainbow around every little event, even the early morning song of a little bird. There's no need to feel sorry for you, Verna. None whatever. You have no time to feel sorry for yourself. You're too busy giving thanks and enjoying things.

Keep it up, Verna. Your sunshiny ways are bringing God's light to a lot of lives—including mine.

Heaven . . . Now, Please

She worded her request carefully. She didn't want God to make any mistakes when he handed back her life plan. Her request went like this:

"Make mine an easy life, Lord. There's no point in wasting a lot of perfectly good time on things like sickness, or injury, or accidents. Everything will work out so much better, don't you see? I'll be able to dedicate full energy to your work without any side tracks.[1] That's so much more efficient, don't you think? I've seen an awful lot of time go to waste because of these kinds of things. As I see it, you need healthy people to carry out your work. I'll be glad to accommodate you if you accommodate me. Think of all the sick people I can minister to if you keep me healthy! That makes sense, doesn't it?

"Oh, and another thing: I'd appreciate it if I never had any cause to become angry, or depressed, or disap-

1. Rom. 8:28.

43

pointed.[2] It would take too much energy away from the Lord's work to deal with these messy items. Wipe my agenda clean, please. I want nothing but blue skies and sunshine in my life so it will be truly 'set apart' for the work you have for me.[3]

"And keep me from making any mistakes . . . and from sinning and all that confession/restoration routine. That kind of thing takes lots of mental energy I could channel other places. Besides, I want other people to look to me as an example of victorious Christianity.[4]

"That reminds me, I'd also like to have a special kind of weather where I work and live. Snowstorms have a way of putting a halt to your business. When cars can't even leave the driveway for church, it's almost impossible for 'the work of God' to go on. Seventy-two degrees will be just fine, with a slight breeze, and sunshine. It makes the saints happier.[5] And let it rain only on the corn fields . . . in the spring . . . at night.

"I'd also appreciate it if no members of my family ever got sick or died. Those things take too much time and money, and clearly detract from weightier matters. Also, it sure would help if we had all the money we need without working for it.[6] Can't you see how the time spent working at a secular job could be put to better use—more spiritually beneficial use?

"There's also the matter of natural disasters. If you really want to see me accomplish anything for the kingdom, keep floods and fires and the like from touching

2. Isa. 26:3.
3. John 16:33.
4. 1 John 1:9–10.
5. 1 Tim. 6:6.
6. Gen. 3:17.

my territory.[7] Nothing could slow things down more than having to stop and build a new church or home because a tornado got sidetracked.

"I think you get the picture, don't you? What I'm basically saying is that the 'work of God' in my little corner of earth can really move ahead if you simply clear the way of all distractions. Actually, this could be the start of something big—an altogether new order. Once you understand how all these things have hindered your work down here, maybe you will see fit to remove them."[8]

Then she got up and went to work . . . and discovered . . . his ways were not her ways . . . and eventually . . . that his were best . . . and it was good.

7. Isa. 43:2.
8. 2 Cor. 12:9.

"I Stand at the Door . . ."

They came together for their weekly Bible study as usual. June, Carrie, and Pat. At least it had begun as a Bible study three years ago, but if you were to ask what their purpose was in gathering today, they may have to think a few minutes.

Christ was in the midst of them as he had promised, and as their unseen guest, he observed with sorrow the progress of the Bible study.

"What's for lunch?" asked Carrie, dropping her new Bible on the lamp table with a thud. "I would have come earlier to help you," she prattled on, "but Curtie has been teething so, and you know how it is."

The next fifteen minutes were filled by a running account of the varied ailments of her two children. Her friends acknowledged each with understanding nods between sips of coffee.

Carrie was a brisk, vivacious sort of woman who made friends easily and lost them even more easily, but she had been a nice addition to the group all the same.

June interrupted the flow of words by injecting a few stories about her own children, spicing things up with a complete review of their medical history. This done, she delved happily into the remains of the lasagna and turned the floor over to the next taker.

Pat stifled a yawn, slid her spoon into the sugar bowl for the second time, and dumped the shimmering crystals into her steaming cup as she proceeded to break the news of her new carpet. After that came tales of camping trips she and Don had taken. Feeling that she had properly one-upped her friends, she settled back to enjoy the mound of fruit salad heaped on her plate.

As a matter of fact, June had served a delicious luncheon, to be surpassed only by the one she would eat next week at Pat's home. "Christian fellowship is really great," she mused, and proceeded to launch into a full-scale discussion of the new city sewer system and how it would affect them.

Christ waited . . . time passed . . . Bibles were untouched (Pat even forgot hers) and no move was made to make him feel at home. No matter. They couldn't very well discuss what wasn't theirs, and the joy of the Lord was not theirs.

Between her second and third cups of coffee, Pat timidly mentioned that her little boy, Tim, had recently accepted Christ. Her two friends grew visibly edgy and nervous. They couldn't seem to think of an appropriate response. Pat quickly climbed back into her shell of respectability . . . but Christ knew there was hope.

The trio had each attended church faithfully since childhood. They gave generously of their time and money, and even served on committees. What's more, they were genuinely born-again ones—but not so you'd notice it.

"Faith is a private thing," June would state flatly if

anyone seemed to want to talk of the goodness of the Lord, and most of her friends agreed. Corpses, they were . . . alive and well in the physical sense, but corpses. The walking dead.

Down the street a few houses, another meeting was taking place. Carol had some overwhelming problems in her home and needed help badly. Her neighbor, Thelma, seemed so understanding. She was pretty religious, but she didn't jam anything down your throat, so it was safe to visit with her. Carol had spilled many tears on Thelma's table, and she was about to do so again. She really shouldn't, because Thelma had enough problems of her own what with Tommy being crippled and all. But somehow she could handle it and Carol couldn't. Thelma wiped her floury hands and reached for two cups. "I can only offer you a cup of coffee," she apologized.

But she offered so much more, that day and in the days to come. Love, acceptance, comfort, and eventually, Christ.

And he was in the midst of them as he had promised. And the Word was opened, and the seed found fertile soil. And all she could offer was a cup of coffee.

See How They Run

The circus was in town, and Thelma Christian had a front-row seat. She never missed a performance. As she put it, "If I'm not there, who'll take my place?"

She spotted her own family in the first ring. All four kids were waving, and so was Ken. Always waving, that bunch. Either coming or going. "Hello, kids." "Good-by, kids." "Hello, Ken." "Good-by, Ken." "Time for devotions? Not today, dear."

Thelma was organized. She had schedules posted all over the kitchen to remind her of upcoming events. Her husband's schedule was the easiest—he was gone every night. In the door—out the door. "See you later." "Bye, dear." "Did you pay the phone bill?" "Where are my new shoestrings?" "Why wasn't the laundry folded?"

"Bye, dear." "Yes, yesterday." "In the drawer." "I'll do it today." Communication was important in Thelma's family.

In the second ring, Thelma recognized several mem-

49

bers of her church. Everyone was scurrying in tight little circles. They were busy. So active. Thelma's phone rang incessantly, and she couldn't seem to say no. Who else would do it?

Her days were filled with committee meetings, luncheons, and grocery trips. Her nights were crowded with banquets and ball teams. The pastor seemed so pleased. "You can count on Thelma," he would say within earshot. Last year she had won a Bible for perfect attendance.

The third ring glittered with a thousand sparkling lights. Feminine voices rose from the half-dark of the arena, and Thelma recognized them as her friends and neighbors. She always made time to socialize. Communication was very important to her. ("Hi, Mom." "Bye, Mom." "What's for dinner, Mom?")

Suddenly the lights flickered. Darkness dropped on the audience. Voices drowned in a sea of black, and the ringmaster assured them that the lights would be fixed in short order. Thelma relaxed in the darkness and realized how tired she was. She slipped out of her seat and headed for home.

Once there, she walked over to straighten her dresser before climbing in bed. She scooped up a dusty stack of books. Her gift Bible was among them. The spot where it had lain was shiny and clean.

Poor Thelma. Her foundations were crumbling, and she was too blind to see the damage. Too preoccupied to repair the bearing wall. Too busy.

The wise woman builds her house,
but with her own hands the foolish one tears hers down.
[Prov. 14:1]

Quiet Time—Why Should I?

I was twenty-five years old, and a mother of three small children. In all sincerity, I asked a missionary wife about the value of spending time in God's presence every day—of reading the Bible every day. I wanted her to agree with my persuasion that all of the urging from the pulpit to read the Bible and pray daily was just so much "sermon filler." After all, hadn't I been in church since I was a child—sometimes three times a week, sometimes more? Didn't I *hear* the Word of God enough? I felt that was sufficient. She didn't agree. And she was right.

Today, twenty years later, personal worship is becoming more vital than the food I eat. In the "quiet times" I have discovered a God who walks with me, and talks with me . . . a God who tells me I am his own. And it is joy unspeakable and full of glory. Now, our time together in the inner sanctum is priceless. Why?

Because the intervening years have been a schoolroom, teaching me that second-hand sermons will never take the place of intimate worship time and personal Bible study. King David must have known that too. And he wrote a song with 176 verses (Ps. 119) to remind himself and us of the importance of God's precepts, statutes, commands, laws, decrees . . . his words. I wonder if David had to learn the importance of the quiet place the hard way too?

Must we all learn . . . the hard way . . . that we *need* a quiet place . . . to worship him . . . to pause at the foot of the throne (Ps. 11:4) and look into the face of the Christ who loved us and who continues to love us (Jer. 31:3) . . . to feel the loving smile of a living Savior who continually speaks to the Father on our behalf (Rom. 8:34) . . . to sense the sunlight of his presence filtering through the clutter of our days and sending heat waves into our sometimes cold world (Matt. 11:28).

We need a quiet time . . . to *enjoy* our Lord, the faithful lover of our souls, and bask in his presence and open our hearts in adoration and praise . . . because he's teaching us who he is (1 John 2:27), and we're liking what we see.

There, in the quiet place, we can sing praises to him as we enter the Holy of Holies (Ps. 108:1–3). We can enter his gates with thanksgiving, his courts with praise (Ps. 100:4).

In the quiet place, we have permission to simply *listen* . . . to prepare the soul to pay homage to the King . . . to let the lyrics of meditative music guide our thoughts and quiet our souls . . . to *read* a portion of Scripture aloud, engraving the words on the air, and confessing the truth with our mouths. We have permission to listen to Scripture read by another on tape, and meditate afterward (Ps. 119:15). And if the soul is bruised, we may enter quietly and simply *rest* in his presence at first. This, for the Christian, is entry into the presence of God in vital, meaningful worship. Sometimes it will be exuberant, sometimes silent. He hasn't handed us an order of worship to follow. And I'm grateful.

A hushed time with God always involves *confession.* In the quiet place we approach the throne in perfect confidence that our confessed sin will be forgiven upon request and we will be restored at once to that comfortable place of fullest fellowship. The Spirit reminds us, nudges us, and urges us to see ourselves as God sees us, and to confess (1 John 1:9–10). Here, we are cleansed, forgiven, and enabled to go on. And we're reminded that Christ died to free us from bondage to continual sinning (1 John 3:9). Here we see the cross, and picture our confessed sin nailed to it. We accept our very expensive freedom, and are grateful.

It is in the quiet place, beside the still waters, that we can *ask* and *receive* (1 John 3:22). He teaches us not to be afraid to ask anything of him. And when we don't know what or how to ask, we can be quiet and accept the promised ministry of the Spirit to interpret the longings of our hearts to the Father in an acceptable way (Rom. 8:26). We ask, knowing that he goes to work on behalf of the request immediately, in his way, in his time. And that's good, because he sees the whole picture and we don't.

In the quiet place, battle takes place: against the world system, the pull of the flesh, and Satan himself. Dressed in full armor (Eph. 6:10–17), we take the offensive against the limited power of Satan in the lives of those we love (Eph. 6:18). God's attention is brought to bear on certain situations, and hedges of protection are built. Here, victories are won and lives rebuilt and redirected. Here, we take authority as a soldier of the Lord on the front lines of conflict.

It is here, in the quiet place, that God breaks the alabaster box and pours the fragrance of Christ into our lives, and makes it a sweet aroma to a world geared to self-destruct (2 Cor. 2:14).

Here, in the quiet place, our rough edges are polished, the cords of love strengthened, the channels of communication opened, the windows of heaven thrown open, and the soul restored. Here, sometimes in no more than twenty minutes, God communes with his creature and the creature with God.

And I have stopped asking, "Why should I?"

Come . . . Meditate with Me

There are lots of ways to enjoy a personal relationship with the Lord: prayer, singing Scripture back to him, and reading his Word, to name a few. But let's consider the power-packed benefits of meditation on biblical truth. Completely ignoring Webster's definitions, let's define meditation in our terms. To meditate is to dwell at length on a thought or thoughts. It is to set that thought on a revolving pedestal in your mind, and look at it again and again from all angles. But there's more. To meditate is to focus on one area to the exclusion of other areas. And when it comes to the Christian, meditation also includes allowing the truth meditated upon to pierce the heart and ultimately to make a whole-life difference.

Experts on mind control tell us we *can* control our thoughts and what we meditate upon, thereby ultimately controlling our mood and our character. In the light of this, it would seem only logical to be cautious about the thoughts we decide to meditate on. We have lots of choices: problems or solutions. Sorrows or joys. Road-blocks or possibilities. Truth or untruth. One road leads to whole new sets of problems. The other to peace. The choice is ours—every moment, every day.

Meditation is a powerful tool for good when biblical truth is the object of meditation. When God's truth becomes absorbed into our systems we begin to change and grow, like a flower receiving the right kind of nutrients. Truth is the Christian's "rain," and "sunshine," and even "fertilizer." The only difference is, we can never get too much.

Meditation has gotten lost for many of us. For others, it simply is not an activity our temperaments make us gravitate toward. Maybe you think it went out with five-cent ice cream cones. And even if it didn't you question the worth of meditation.

It is true that an activity should not be added to already busy lives just for the sake of adding it. On the other hand, if biblical truth can change life . . .

Consider the benefits of biblical meditation:

1. It guides thought patterns—God's way.
2. It relaxes yet stimulates you.
3. It gives God a chance to really go to work.
4. It blocks out destructive thought patterns.
5. It is an excellent aid to worship.
6. It is a sparkling addition to a personal quiet time gone dry.

With these things in mind, let's consider how to meditate.

Me Meditate? How?

Walking is wonderful. I'm sold on the benefits to the whole person. It's also a great time to meditate. Here's an exercise for you to try the next time you take a fifteen- or thirty-minute walk.

First, slowly read Proverbs 3:5–6 until you know it by memory (or write it on a card). Ask the Holy Spirit to guide you into all the truth contained in the passage.

Begin walking briskly, repeating the verses *slowly* a few times. Then, begin to meditate on one or two words at a time, paraphrasing the truth as you allow God's Word to sink in. Here's an example:

trust in: Believe in. Rely on. Depend on fully. Anchor my lifeboat to. Like a child.

the Lord: Who? God! The creator of this world—of me. The sustainer of the universe. The Almighty who loves me and proved it by providing "so great salvation." My boss. The all-wise one who knows what's ahead.

with all: Not part. Not a little bit. Not a small share. All. If I trust with a part I am mistrusting with all the rest. He doesn't want halfhearted allegiance from me. Fullhearted trust. I can trust him with everything. I don't need to hold back.

your heart: The core of my being. Me!

and lean not: Don't depend on, or completely trust or stake my life on . . .

your own understanding: The way I perceive events. My view. It's clouded by prejudice, cultural conditioning, incomplete knowledge. I can't always piece things together.

in all your ways: In everything: my plans, decisions, work, play, worship, relationships. He's talking about *my* ways. I can't do this for anyone else. It's personal.

acknowledge: Give God credit due him. He's in charge. Bow to his authority. Give him room in my life plans. Ask his guidance and direction.

him: God! Give God the honor due him. My master and shepherd.

and he: God himself. Not an angel or a pastor or a friend. Not a book or a leader of a seminar. Not a tape.

will: No doubt about it. This is a promise!

make . . . straight: He will lead me even when I don't realize I'm being led. He will point the way—straighten the road. He will direct me.

your paths: How very personal: *my* paths. He is interested in individual choices and paths.

Thank you, Father.

"Fill Me Up, Lord"

A hungry soul grows weak with malnutrition and begs a crust of bread.

—*Calvin Miller,* The Song

In the beginning . . . *your* beginning of new life in Christ, you were handed a cup of life. It was full then. It is still full, but of different things. What *is* in your cup now? Empty it out and take a look at the contents. What are they? Relationships? Activities? Work? Responsibilities? Christ? Remember how it was . . . in the beginning? When your cup was full of Christ it quenched not only your thirst, but also the thirst of those who surrounded you. It was complete and total nourishment. But somewhere along the way, you began to seek nourishment from other quarters, and though it worked well enough for a quick fix, it didn't last, and the dregs at the bottom of the cup were bitter and tasteless. Not at all like the living water you were used to.

How and when did *Redbook* and *Working Woman* take the place of Bible study? Just when did the nine o'clock movie slip into your usual time for prayer and solitude? Was it an accident that your Sundays became days of rest . . . during the worship hour? When did the starvation begin? When will it end? Look at you . . . look at your cup. Empty cup. Empty soul. Overfed but undernourished. Got to make a change. Time to get back on track. You know where the food is (you have it in six translations!). You know the Life-giver (Christ never altered his stance of love toward you).

Did you open the door to busyness? Did it clamor for your attention—especially after you took a job? Did you put on your blinders and keep repeating, "It really can't matter that much"? Did your tomorrows turn into the todays you planned to do something about it? And did your todays quickly turn into yesterdays that disappeared into the yawning caverns of nevermore? I know the feeling. It's all gray and prickly, and it doesn't go away. For the Christian, the hunger for God's Word and prayer fellowship with him will never entirely go away. Some just get used to the hunger pains.

You will always need cups full of Christ. At salvation, he becomes your life, and forever after he remains available in all his golden fullness.

Established, then: You *are* hungry—maybe starving. You *do* have a full "refrigerator," but haven't made time to open the door. But you want that to change. You're ready. He's ready. You may not have the time now for Bible study and prayer, but some rearranging can change that. Ask yourself:

1. Is there a fifteen-minute activity I perform daily? Can I eliminate that activity and use the time for devotions? (Perhaps a simpler hairdo will do the trick here.)
2. Are there two activities I can combine in such a way that I add fifteen minutes to my day? Example: File your nails while your diesel engine is warming up.
3. Can I double recipes and cut meal preparation in half?
4. Can I make a full pot of coffee once and save the remainder for meals later in the day? (A thermos works wonders here.)
5. Can I fold laundry or iron while the evening news is on?
6. Write your own ideas in this space:

Fifteen minutes—not much—sometimes not enough. But a beginning. It's yours—and it's God's. And he will meet you there, and fill your soul, and nourish your spirit, and quench your thirst for living water. It's his job. And he's good at it. *Read Scripture. Pray. Meditate. Wait on God.*

Here are some practical tips that make devotional times a reality for the busy, sometimes overwhelmed working woman:

1. Walk or ride a bike to work whenever possible. Pray as you go.

2. Get the Bible on cassette (at most Christian bookstores) and listen to Scripture on your way to or from work by using a portable cassette recorder or the tape deck in your car.

3. Get a set of earphones and a player. Listen to a Scripture cassette as you bike, jog, or work in a noisy workplace.

4. Turn on a Scripture cassette as you retire or as you get up.

5. Write your own method here before you forget:

Is Every Morning Monday?

The alarm thundered through my dreams, and another Monday stood front and center, awaiting inspection. I slid sullenly over the edge of the bed and groped my way into my slippers and wrinkled bathrobe. I was forty years old, and for two months I had been working outside my home four days a week—on the heels of *years* of work as full-time wife and mother of three. My comfortable, organized world had turned upside down, and I was trying hard to get used to the distorted picture from the underside.

I was tired all the time, grumpy (to put it mildly), dissatisfied, and my house was a disaster. Problems were mounting faster than they were being solved, and I wrestled daily with a schedule that refused to be controlled.

When I took my job, I was one of those "do-almost-everything" women. I cleaned the two-story farmhouse virtually by myself, fixed all the meals, washed the clothes of my husband and three teen-agers, baked frequently, entertained, sewed, and juggled several church and school jobs. Both my culture and my church had taught me that caring for my home and family was my main function. I interpreted this to mean that I was to do almost everything without aid. And, except for minimal help from the kids, I did. After all, they had sports and homework, and my husband had plenty to do also. This division of duties was functional—until I took an outside job.

History told me families had worked together at making a living for centuries—until industrialization and stable prices made it possible for one man to support himself plus several others. But now, inflation was changing all that, and, because I had no pattern to follow, I was forced to cut my own.

For sixteen years I had been there to catch my family when they fell. I had trained them to depend on me instead of themselves. When I first began chopping four days out of my week to earn wages and help with expenses, I did not adjust my home responsibilities downward or delegate outward, nor did my family adjust their expectations of me. And that formula—the same things being done in the same way, by me—didn't work anymore.

During this difficult time of adjustment, well-meaning Christian women friends expressed disappointment in my working, saying I previously had been such a good example for them. *Example of what?* I wondered. *Could working make me any less of a Christian model?*

Making insidious journeys into my working days, guilt began pushing me to excel—at great personal expense. I tried hard not to let anything or anyone "suffer" because I was working, even though I worked to help keep their home afloat. At this point, I was bearing the work adjustment alone (except for the Lord), and these pressures plus my poor attitude made life gray around the edges. I was convinced that working was at best a mistake, at worst, a sin.

It took a few years and a lot of patient work on God's part *and* my family's part to help me come to grips with reality: The preservation of the family can sometimes mean working away from it, and, of itself, working is not a "bad thing" for which one need apologize.

Measurable progress began when I let go of some home responsibilities and distributed them among family members. We all needed reeducation, and it didn't come easily. I began as slowly as possible, at first delegating small chores, then gradually adding more. I worked toward an even distribution of housework, trying not to force instant adjustment on anyone.

As for myself, I *had* to scale down my definition of *clean*. I had to learn to look through a dirty window and see the view instead of the spatters. (This wasn't easy in a neighborhood where clean windows were next to godliness.) One of the most exciting changes came within myself as I discovered that this inevitable upheaval in our work patterns was good preparation for a tomorrow that would not resemble our yesterdays: My son would probably marry a woman who worked (and ran her home). My girls would probably be expected by their husbands and society to work (and run a home). They needed a work pattern. I began to see my working as a positive force in molding my children for their actual futures— not one I dreamed up for them. This brought great internal relief to me and a force of conviction to my efforts at delegating.

Over a period of time, God helped my family and me to readjust our expectations of each other and redirect our work schedules. I was eventually able to earn money from my home instead of outside it. That, in itself, solved many problems. As the children were able, they took paying jobs and shared expenses as well as home care. I saw the futility of bearing unfounded guilt for "home desertion" and began to enjoy a strange, sweet satisfaction. After all, wasn't I in a generation of Christian women who were breaking in brand new shoes for our daughters? Pioneer efforts are always unnerving, but usually rewarding. I hope my children can build on the framework I've laid and improve greatly on my methods.

For me—for us—attitude adjustments and shifting workloads have come in lurches and starts. But they *have* come. And the family under my roof is better prepared for the second phase of life than they would have been had I not worked. The Andersen family BW (before work) was too dependent on me, and it was my fault. The Andersen family AW (after work) won't fall apart if I get sick or die. The kids are also better prepared for marriage and not so apt needlessly to depend on their partners. My coddled darlings of yesterday are self-sufficient!

I hope the women following in my footsteps into the waves of the twenty-first century will point to me and my co-workers in pride because we tested the water and told them what it felt like. And because we did it, with God's help, rather well.

Plain Talk to Wives Who Work

"Yes, I work full time outside the home, and I have a family too, but I can take care of the home front by myself. Or can I?"

Well, I suppose I can give it a try. After all, Carol down the street does (but she's a nervous wreck). Sue does (but she's forgotten the names of her kids). Marti does too (but her husband left her when she convinced him that kissing was out of style).

If these women had learned to delegate, they might be managing a job and home much better. Abigail knew how to entrust functions to others (see 1 Sam. 25:19). Sarah didn't try to do all the cooking for Abraham's bunch either. And Queen Esther prepared banquets fit for a king, but not without help. True, these women undoubtedly had servants or slaves. Even so, you are not without resources if your husband and children are interested in your welfare. And sharing work with them as they are able has benefits for all of you.

Delegating will decrease your workload and give you more time. And the work does get done (usually!), even if it isn't quite the way you would do it. Delegating minimizes frustration because you have taken charge of managing your home rather than allowing it to manage you. Delegating goes a long way toward eliminating guilt, because you *are* doing a good job.

Delegating the work of the home also has some pluses for your family. Your husband and children will enjoy a more energetic wife and mother who has time to be fun once in a while.

Delegating work spreads the accountability. This prepares children for the future—a future that may include working spouses. Christian moms will have time for building their relationships with God.

Sharing home responsibilities with your husband will give him the opportunity to set the tone for cheerful cooperation—a model your children need.

As your family learns to share the many aspects of running a household, they will begin to view mother as a member of the team—not as a housemaid who "does it all but frowns a lot." Your children will be better able to cope with the unexpected burden of parental illness. And your husband will be prepared to take care of things if the need arises.

In a very real sense, delegating is one answer to coping with rapidly changing family patterns. It will help families of today make the transition into tomorrow without bearing the burden of yesterday's expectations.

Beatitudes for the Workplace

Blessed (happy and to be emulated) is the woman who willingly exchanges her warm bed for the sometimes cold challenges of a new day, for she will be glad she did.

How long will you lie there, you sluggard?
When will you get up from your sleep?
A little sleep, a little slumber,
a little folding of the hands to rest—
and poverty will come on you like a bandit. . . . [Prov. 6:9–11]

Blessed is the woman who arrives on time and sets about her work with diligence and disciplined determination. Her work will tend to be satisfying both to her *and* to her employer.

Lazy hands make a man poor,
but diligent hands bring wealth. [Prov. 10:4]

70

Blessed is the woman who turns down overdoses of sugar at break time in exchange for an alert mind and an energetic body. All she has to lose is pounds and lethargy. And she stands to gain the respect of her employer and co-workers for exercising a restraint that pays off.

Do not join those who drink too much wine
　　or gorge themselves on meat,
for drunkards and gluttons become poor,
　　and drowsiness clothes them in rags. [Prov. 23:20]

Blessed is the working woman who volunteers to bring a co-worker or an employer some refreshment on her way back from the cafeteria (or coffee machine). She shall deserve gratitude and thanks. But more than that, she shall be doing as Christ would do—particularly if she brings coffee to someone who despitefully uses her.

He who tends a fig tree will eat its fruit,
　　and he who looks after his master will be honored.
　　　[Prov. 27:18]

Blessed and respected is the Christian woman who tactfully supervises other workers in the same way she would want to be supervised. She will merit great favor and elicit the undying curiosity of those under her who wonder why she bothers.

Like a roaring lion or a charging bear
　　is a wicked man ruling over a helpless people.
A tyrannical ruler lacks judgment,
　　but he who hates ill-gotten gain will enjoy a long life.
　　　[Prov. 28:15–16]

Blessed is the discerning woman who knows that reading her Bible during break or during work hours usually generates unnecessary antagonism, especially when the boss is in full view, tearing his or her hair out because work is days behind schedule. She knows that her life message in the workplace will be evidence enough that she has been with God in private.

> When Moses came down from Mount Sinai with the two tablets of the Testimony in his hands, he was not aware that his face was radiant because he had spoken with the LORD. [Exod. 34:29]

Truly blessed and wise is the woman who studies the Proverbs relating to work,* for she will not be found among those unfortunates who view each working day as wasted time because they aren't "doing something spiritual." She will understand that work was the first gift God gave the first human (*before* the curse), probably because he knew how much good it would do him.

> The LORD God took the man and put him in the Garden of Eden to work it and take care of it. [Gen. 2:15]

Blessed is the motivated woman who forgets to watch the clock because she's watching her work instead. She shall be highly regarded and used as an example by observant employers.

> She gets up while it is still dark;
>   she provides food for her family
>   and portions for her servant girls.
> She watches over the affairs of her household
>   and does not eat the bread of idleness. [Prov. 31:15, 27]

*On her own time.

Blessed is the Christian woman who refuses to enter into gossip about her employer or co-workers, for she shall be trusted above her fellows.

If anyone considers himself religious and yet does not keep a tight rein on his tongue, he deceives himself and his religion is worthless. [James 1:26]

A gossip betrays a confidence,
   but a trustworthy man keeps a secret. [Prov. 11:13]

Blessed and all too rare is the woman who understands that diligence, honesty, thoughtfulness, efficiency, and creative alertness are her primary tools for witness in the workplace, and that leaving tracts in the coffee-break area can be as fruitless as trying to feed steaks to goldfish.

Blessed is the woman whose antenna is out to people with special needs. She can generally develop a bond of friendship and find opportunities *over lunch* or *after hours* to administer Christ-like concern.

Blessed and appreciated is the woman who is loyal and respectful to her employer and company for Christ's sake, for she will usually be among the first to be considered for a promotion or a raise. And even if she isn't, she can experience inner peace because her focus is higher than an executive suite.

Blessed is the woman who seeks to expand and improve her skills, for who knows what good things are in store for her!

Do you see a man skilled in his work?
   He will serve before kings;
   he will not serve before obscure men. [Prov. 22:29]

Blessed is the woman who doesn't compose her letter of resignation every time things get "hot." She shall be strengthened by knowing "that it takes a breeze to make a banner speak" (Calvin Miller, *The Song*).

Blessed is the woman who has enough common sense to stop feeding truth to someone who has never yet been hungry. She will not become a person co-workers avoid.

But in your hearts set apart Christ as Lord. Always be prepared to give an answer to everyone who asks you to give the reason for the hope that you have. But do this with gentleness and respect, keeping a clear conscience, so that those who speak maliciously against your good behavior in Christ may be ashamed of their slander. [1 Peter 3:15–16]

A Conversation with God

Just a part of your plan today, Father? Is that all I get
to see—just this odd-shaped puzzle piece of a happening?
But it doesn't look like it will fit. Not from my angle.
I would have had it happen another way.

Why do you give me such little windows to see
through, Father? I like bay windows and skylights so
much better. I like to look way ahead and be able to
make plans around ordered, expected events. I like to fit
them neatly and precisely into my schedule and make
sure there are no surprises—no pieces that don't fit. Last-
minute emergencies and unexpected moves are not for
me.

It's so upsetting, Father, to have surprises dumped in
my lap when I'm not ready. It makes me feel so defense-
less and, yes, so angry sometimes. Like the day guests
dropped in when both my refrigerator *and* my billfold
were empty. Yet a Scripture verse kept writing itself on
my mind, "All things work together for good to them

that love God. . . ." That's me, Father! I *do* love you. But we certainly don't see eye to eye sometimes. I suppose it's me that needs the glasses.

It wouldn't be so bad if the surprises were always happy. But take last week. I was committed up to my ears, and two friends had personal tragedies. I had nothing left to give, yet I felt they needed me. What about that, Father? What—they really needed only you? You took me out of the way on purpose? Oh.

I still say things could be more orderly. Tragedies could fall in one particular week of the year, and babies and weddings in another. Illness could be reserved for January so everyone's Christmas would be bright. Don't you see, Father? It would be so neat that way. Men could lose jobs, and women babies, in April. Raises and twins would come in May. Couldn't it be worked out? Why not avoid those crisscross events that bring us to the end of ourselves? What—because that's one of the purposes? Your strength begins where our weakness leaves off? If that's so, then I don't need ordered events, do I? I just need you. I *have* you!

A Sermon in Song

I stepped outside to mail a letter, and sunlight laid a glittering path between me and the mailbox. It was the middle of November—the waiting room of winter—and all the birds were supposed to have flown south. Then what was the chattering I heard in the tops of our giant maples? I looked up and saw a bird convention! Hundreds of birds had congregated happily in the bare but sunny treetops, and they seemed to be having a celebration. About what I didn't know. Their voices twittered and trilled in a symphonic harmony, and I found myself wanting to say, "Stop that! Don't you know what a sad world we live in? Aren't you aware of all the suffering going on, and the bitter tears cried under roofs on this very street just this morning?" I wanted to remind them of the boy in our neighborhood who had been killed last summer, and of another who had taken his own life. I wanted them to remember fifteen-year-old Mike who may never use his legs again because of a diving accident.

I frowned at the letter in my hands with a hot shame. In this case, I had been the one to hurt, and apology was overdue and wrung out of a stubborn heart. What right did those birds have to sing? I wanted to squeeze their happiness into a bucket of tears and mold their cheery voices into waxen frowns more appropriate to the world I was a part of. I almost wanted to change their song to a funeral dirge, and drape their energetic melody in black flags of doom. After all, you don't sing allelujahs at funerals! And you don't congratulate a world that seems gripped in a terminal illness, do you?

But the birds kept singing. And the sun kept shining. I stopped for a few minutes and watched, and found myself smiling in spite of myself. I was lifted, and happier. The hurting letter in my hand didn't burn so much. What were the words of their song, I wondered. Surely God knew. Maybe it was a private language between them. It was beautiful—lilting—joyous. I lifted my head up, past the cars on the street, past the birds, and beyond the skeletal treetops. I lifted my eyes. And I prayed.

Musical notes continued to sift down through naked branches, and a breeze bore them down the street where the tears had been, and scattered them over the home enduring anguish. It was a message of eternal hope—a reminder that God is here and now to sustain and in the future for a glorious forever.

The bird convention moved on. I expect they had an itinerary. I was glad they had stopped here—busy, little, singing bodies—full-throated messengers of a love that will never, never die.

I put my letter of apology in the mailbox, lifted the little red flag, and ignored the hot tears carving valleys down my cheeks.

The Note

I burst into God's throne room without the usual knock or prescribed passwords. A storm of emotion boiled as I raised my fist throneward and shouted, "No more! No more of this trial, Lord. I've tried everything, and I can't handle it!" Then I collapsed in a heap at the foot of the cross which served as a gateway to the throne, and sobbed. Great black tears were wrung out of craters somewhere deep inside and careened down my cheeks. I talked as I cried, knowing he could still understand—feeling there was some escape after all. I pounded my fists against the throne-room floor in an agony of pain and frustration as I told him my story.

It had begun some four or five years earlier, when an "irregular person" (a term coined by Joyce Landorf) invaded my life. Then began the torment of dealing on a routine basis with a spirit that collided head-on with all my values and prefabricated notions of right and wrong. One by one, my strongholds were attacked—gave way.

Bit by bit, my confidence drained. Step by step I entered the no-man's-land of "I can't deal with this person!" But I always stumbled away from the skirmishes nursing the belief that I really *must* have it in me *somewhere*. If I could just work at it harder, do more, be clearer and wiser. I continued to try, and kept getting battle-scarred. The "trophies" were always awarded to my irregular opponent who consistently won nearly every encounter. I was bruised—bleeding. But I still had not come to the end of my supposed resources until I found the note. It was meant for me. It was an exposé of a hurting heart. Wounds I had inflicted were leaving scars. That moment, I began to face the truth I had avoided. I was the irregular person in her life too.

The note was the beginning of the end for me. It crashed through pride and arrogance, dealing a fatal blow to self-sufficiency. That's when I ran to the throne room for a hearing.

I stayed there a long time—at the feet of Jesus. Eternities passed as I confessed sin in raw, honest terms, and asked for a fresh touch from his spirit to mine. When the storm subsided and I found the strength to raise the eyes of my soul, they rested, as it were, on the Master, who was smiling his forgiveness. A bright beam of love lay across my shoulders where the burden had been.

I realized I had done something I'd never really done before. From the depths of my being, I had confessed my complete inability to live "the good Christian life" in my own strength. I had turned myself over completely and unreservedly into his care and had given him permission to run the show.

The change in my responses was almost immediate. Love flowed from my inner being toward my irregular person as well as to others. In coming days, joy filled my cup consistently, to a much larger measure than ever before. Courage to witness did not need to be mustered. It was inside me, pushing its way out.

During the coming days, I discovered that suddenly *nothing* meant as much as maintaining this close walk with my Lord. Peace flowed in and around my spirit in unfamiliar surges.

I didn't try to label and box this special growth time with God—I didn't have to. He was God, and he could do what he chose, when he chose to do it. It needed no label.

Nearly thirty years of straining to "do this" and "don't do that" had culminated in a life-shaking realization that Christ had not only saved me, but also was in charge of my growth. I could no more "grow" myself up in the Christian life than I could save myself from my sins. He had been waiting for a broken, contrite heart *all the time*. He wanted me to stop saying, "Lord, what can I do *for* you?" and start saying, "Lord, what can you do *through* me?" He wanted me to take my hands off my spiritual life and admit that accomplishing something spiritual in me was his work.

It was almost like being born again to realize that God's Holy Spirit had filled and enabled me in response to unconditional surrender. The difference was day and night. I wanted to tell everybody, but soon discovered that everybody was not ready to listen, just as I had not been. I cautiously told two pastors' wives and one pastor. They did not grasp what I meant. I crept back into my shell and simply enjoyed God. It was enough. To each in his own time come brokenness, repentance, and then personal quickening by the Holy Spirit of power—daybreak on the soul.

The Wall

A wall of unspoken words and unshared experiences stood between my would-be friend and me. It was thick, and solid, and visible only to us—most of the time. I didn't like it. She didn't like it. It was ugly. It was wide. It seemed impregnable. And for a long time, I thought it was always going to be there.

The wall divided us, even when we worked and worshiped side by side. It kept us from open, honest encounters, and pigeonholed our words into socially correct little essays on the weather and world affairs—safe talk. We talked "around" each other, always missing the mark—never quite walking through the misty wall of veiled words into the sun. We touched physically only when necessary, and then only over the wall of protection—briefly—correctly—coldly.

I wanted it to be different, and I think she did too. When would it begin to happen, and where would it begin to end? And how?

82

Prickly vines had grown into the crevices between the stones, covering every chink. Thorns ran helter-skelter across the top edge. They bothered us only when we both got too close to the wall, and that wasn't often.

The wall had been there so long we were almost used to it—the way an invalid gets used to pain. Actually, we didn't know how to relate without the wall. In a way, it shielded us from the danger of honest exposure and wall-breaking repentance. It stood as a proud testimony to a shrunken relationship that pleased the Adversary.

Almost from the first, we both worked at erecting the wall. Prejudiced initial impressions laid the foundation. Later, personality clashes came and more stones were added to the wall. A calcified build-up of suspicion, mistrust, and unrealistic expectations mortared the stones together tightly. Intermittent doses of critical response and anger eventually built a wall so high neither one of us could scale it. And anger boiled just below the surface.

At least we were safe from each other, even though we had to be around each other a lot. But safety brought with it an unexpected loneliness and sense of estrangement when we were together. Could it be that we *needed* the fellowship of each other? The loneliness eventually brought another surprise: an overwhelming desire to break down the wall—destroy it forever.

God knew I didn't have the heart. He knew I throbbed with fear and inadequacy and a big dose of stubborn reluctance. I told him plainly there was no reason I should be the first one. At first, I told him I couldn't—wouldn't. And so, for a while, the wall remained, spoiling contact after contact.

Finally, there came a day I knew the wall must go. It had taken too big a toll already. It had come to a point where in a crowded room we could feel the presence of each other stronger than the presence of others in the room. I had to make a move.

God gave me encouragement, saying in his word,

Wait for the LORD;
   be strong and take heart
   and wait for the LORD. [Ps. 27:14]

And he chastised me by reminding me that "if anyone says, 'I love God,' yet hates his brother, he is a liar. For anyone who does not love his brother, whom he has seen, cannot love God, whom he has not seen" (1 John 4:20). I knew this meant "sisters" too.

A key word kept coming to mind as I thought about what might tear down the wall. Love . . . God's love in sending his Son . . . Christ's love in doing the Father's will. The love that God poured all over us "while we were yet sinners." That's the kind of love that tears down walls of separation—the only kind that would tear this wall down. Supernatural love is the "power tool" God uses to penetrate walls every day. But how could I get hold of that kind of love? I could try to produce it myself. But I'd tried that route, and had fallen on my face so quickly I was stunned. I was learning not to rely on *my* strength when it came to spiritual matters.

What was left? God seemed to point time and time again to the scriptural principle of abiding in Christ (John 15). Over and over again this spiritual law was becoming a touchstone for every problem. He was teaching me that "apart from *me* you can do *nothing*." And at the same time, he was saying that "I can do everything through him [Christ] who gives me strength." The difference between impotence and power lay in the extent to which I learned to "abide in Christ," or rest in him, trust in him, commit to him. No matter what the problem, he became my solution. My most important spiritual work, as I saw it, was to abide, or lean this dividing wall into his almighty arms and receive the spiritual nourishment to move ahead in his love—not mine.

The wall of estrangement and isolation had been built over a period of time—slowly—one stone at a time. I could not expect it to fall down like the walls of Jericho. I also knew that the whole affair might not work out exactly the way I planned, because God is God. There was no guarantee that this person would fully appreciate or respond to my loving her. But I was still responsible for obeying Christ's mandate to "love one another as I have loved you." There it was: the order, and the ammunition to carry out the order. *His* persistent, irresistible love would take it from there. I was to allow him to love her through me.

God's love—it had torn down strongholds in a million hearts already. Is anything too hard for God?

In my spirit, I watched a crack begin at the top of the wall and run all the way down to the foundation. And I walked over and picked up the phone. It had begun.

Healing at "First Church"

It was hot and still in Philippi this afternoon. The believers were especially excited about their meeting because they would be listening to a letter from Paul, their beloved brother in the Lord. Travelers through Philippi had brought rumors that Paul was in jail at Rome, and the anxious believers wondered what to expect from this letter.

The jailer, together with his wife and household, sat at rapt attention. This man, Paul, had introduced them to a Christ who had revolutionized their lives. And he had done it while in prison! Now Paul was in jail again, and they yearned to hear about him.

Clement sat quietly to the side, stroking his beard. The overseers and deacons talked among themselves, deciding who should read the letter.

Lydia was composed, but concerned. She was the charter member of the church at Philippi and the first to meet Paul. He meant much to her.

Euodia and Syntyche sat uneasily across a sort of aisleway from each other. Neither would look at the other. They had disagreed rather violently on a matter lately, and since then had avoided each other. The few feet between them was alive with tension, ready to ignite.

An overseer began to read, "I thank my God every time I remember you. In all my prayers for all of you, I always pray with joy because of your partnership in the gospel. . . ." He read on, but tears blurred his vision. Euodia cleared her throat and twisted her hands in her skirts. Syntyche squirmed.

"Whatever happens," the letter went on, "conduct yourselves in a manner worthy of the gospel of Christ." Euodia turned to hide the tears. She barely heard the next sentence: "Then, . . . I will know that you stand firm in one spirit, contending as one man. . . ." Syntyche compressed her lips and stiffened. ". . . having the same love, being one in the spirit and purpose . . ."

The two women looked toward the door, thinking of escape, and in doing so, their eyes met. ". . . Your attitude should be the same as that of Christ Jesus." Euodia wiped her brow and looked at Epaphroditus, Paul's esteemed friend. Why did he have to bring the letter? She tried to concentrate. "I plead with Euodia and I plead with Syntyche to agree with each other in the Lord." Time stood still and then shattered into a thousand tiny crystals. Forgiveness struggled with pride. "Yes, and I ask you, loyal yokefellow, help these women. . . ."

The three of them heard no more. Syzygus rose and extended his hands to the two women, and they left to discuss the matter. Tears stood on every cheek.

Think and Do

She shivered in the blue chill of an early spring morning and built a fire in the wood stove. As warmth seeped into the room she watched a blanket of sunbeams lay a cozy path across her lap.

Today she was hopeful, joyful, positive. Two days ago, it was not so. Yesterday made all the difference.

Today she was still a bird with a broken wing, thanks to problems which had come galloping in like an unwelcome band of mercenary soldiers.

Today she still had a child who gave her daily pangs of worry—fear—uncertainty.

Today she was still a round peg in a square hole at her church, and every time she moved, it pinched . . . like shoes that never quite fit, but you have to wear them anyway because they're the only pair you have.

Today the money was still tight, and bills were piling up. Yet today was different.

Two days ago, her thoughts had continually dug

around in the murky dungeon of her woes and arranged and rearranged and played with them and indulged them. She had invited Self-pity in, and Discouragement, and a host of surprise guests came along with them: Fear, Doubt, Lack of Self-esteem, and Bitterness. Her house was full. She fed them all, around the clock, and they stayed on and on, until finally when she really began to want them to leave, they wouldn't go. They had planted themselves firmly in her thought house and she was spiraling downward into a self-made den of depressed, defeated thoughts and actions.

Finally, recognizing what she had allowed, thought by thought, she walked to the windows of her thought house, threw them open, and cried out to God. She then turned the full fury of her wrath on one guest at a time, ordering them in the name of her Savior to depart. They didn't want to move at first. Despair and Futility were the first to go—slowly—reluctantly. After that, Discouragement and Doubt left. "We'll be back!" They shook their fists as they left. "No, you won't!" she shouted. And this time, she meant it. After the last one had gone, she slammed and bolted the door against them. Then she got her Bible and began to *believe* what she read: ". . . whatever is true, . . . noble, . . . right, . . . pure, . . . lovely, . . . admirable—if anything is excellent or praiseworthy—*think* about such things. Whatever you have learned or received or heard from me, or seen in me [Paul]—*put it into practice*. And the God of peace will be with you" (Phil. 4:8–9, italics added).

She began inviting a new set of friends to the home of her mind. Each time Doubt or one of his cronies knocked, she would send Faith to the door, and he would turn them away. Faith brought with him Trust, and Peace, and even the unexpected guest, Joy. There were moments of struggle to keep the door shut on her old familiar friends, but she had finally come to realize that she could never, never again allow them even a short visit. They were too dangerous, and her new friends too precious. God was giving her the strength to bring into captivity every thought to the obedience of Christ (2 Cor. 10:5).

And wasn't that just like him?

A Prayer-Talk with God

I've got more troubles than I know what to do with today, Lord. And so has our country. Is this day really just a speck against a backdrop of eternity? Are your stars really brighter during the dark times? It's days like this that make me wonder.

I look at our country's political machinery, and it seems to have gone haywire. Have you seen the headlines? Women openly push for the "right" to kill their own babies before they're born. Couples walk away from marriage commitments and from children to pursue their own selfish interests. Bible clubs and prayer are forced out of public places, and homosexuals are invited in. Energies and monies are expended to promote the very acts you decry—acts that degrade our bodies and bring a slow rotting to our spirits.

There's something else besides the state of the nation that gets me down, Lord. It's the state of me. Why do you, how *can* you keep on loving . . . forgiving . . .

when I seem not to change, not to grow, not to delight in you? It makes me angry and ashamed and defeated to think about me.

Also, there are too many times when the money isn't there and the bills are. Sometimes the kids break my heart, and sometimes I break yours. Some days even your sun seems to be crying great, hot tears of shame over the earth it mothers so tenderly. And the moon broods sullen and angry over this wayward globe in the night watches.

Ah, but then there's you! Praise your holy name that there are oceans of reasons to glory in you and your saving power, your infinite love and incredible, surprising forgiveness patterns.

And the stars! They are always there, aren't they? But when I continually look down, I don't see them. I forget they're there. All I see is the dirt, brown and ugly, and the mud, and the ruts in the road. Maybe if I kept my gaze on you and your stars, the defects on the ground wouldn't loom so large and get all out of proportion.

You've seen it all before, haven't you, Father? And you know the beginning from the end. And in the end you will triumph—hallelujah! I had almost forgotten how temporary our earthly existence is . . . and how long "forever" will be.

Cement my trembling feet in your Word and strengthen my arms for their tasks.

And always, always, Lord, let me see events through your eyes, with glasses labeled "Made in Eternity."

Hard times? Maybe. Sickness? Possibly. Sorrow? Inevitably. Hurt? It will come. Weariness? Always. Joy? Unspeakable. Praise? Unbounding. Thanksgiving? With humility. Peace? Unsurpassed. Hope? A river!

Who but us, your children, can stand with feet rooted

in earth's pain and raise hands and heart to you in authentic love and jubilation of spirit because we know, oh, how we know, the triumph of the inner spirit you've planted inside. And as we feel alternate stabs of pain and joy that go with living on earth, we lift our eyes in very real hope and expectation, for our Redeemer liveth!

Got Any Mountains?

I trudged upward with God's sunshine on my back, kicking up puffy little dust clouds with my tired feet. Violets, resplendent in lavender plumage, smiled up at me from their roadside beds. Sunrays danced dizzily through a shimmering white ball of dandelion seed, and God began working his summer magic inside me.

In an effort to quiet my pounding heart, I pushed my nose deep into the husky fragrance of the gold and blue bouquet of wildflowers in my hand. Cows gathered at the fence, staring silent questions at me, and I resented their intrusion. The pressures of an unruly world had closed relentlessly around me for weeks. Demand had piled upon demand, and no let-up was in sight. Inescapable mandates pushed themselves into my life and I was pushing back—hard. "Don't do this to me, Lord. You know I can't take it."

The Lord did not comfort me by telling me that I could. In the midst of climbing the highest mountain, my strength was spent. I pressed forward as if in a fog. I could not meet the next demand. And I didn't.

But moments before I had to face it—only moments—he sent a noticeable physical refreshing. I was able to take the next step . . . and the next . . . and the next. When I finally crossed that mountain, I looked ahead and saw another—and my heart failed me. "I can't do it, Lord," my soul cried. "Remove the mountain." When I lifted tear-filled eyes, the mountain was still there. I wanted to retreat, to run away. But the path led only ahead. The Lord's reply to Gideon rang in my ears, "Go in the strength you have. Am *I* not sending you?"

When I looked ahead, I saw only briars and rocks lining the path up the mountain. My strength and resolve were all gone. But then I turned around, and I saw what a long way I had come. Hope leaped alive, and I recalled his promise never to leave me nor forsake me. I looked up to my Resource and saw his limitless power. Then I took the next step, and the next. One by one, the steps reduced the height of the mountain. I'm halfway up now, and I know I'll make it.

Christian friend, my mountain is no bigger than yours—it's only in a different place. My resource is no different from yours—for God is everywhere present. And he specializes in things thought impossible. No mountain is too big for you and him.

I wonder . . . was I called to climb the mountain first in order to spy out the land for you?

No Time for Sunsets

Looking up from my work, I was just in time to catch the grand finale of what must have been a really spectacular sunset. A thought gently urged itself forward from somewhere in my center being, and I knew I really could have taken time for the celestial show. But the "Martha" in me replied stoutly, "Why should I? Besides, how *can* I?" Watching sunsets won't get my dishes done, or the laundry folded. It won't tuck kids in bed or bathe them. The car needs washing, too. And my flowers have to be watered. Sunset watchers just aren't achievers. At least by some standards. They frankly don't seem to worry about getting things done—at least not all that much. That's no way to get on top of things, is it?

It was a great idea, and I appreciated the thought. Actually, I love a good sunset as much as some people love a hot fudge sundae. But how could I explain a thing like that to my friends? "Sorry, I was late for the committee meeting because I was watching the sunset." And

96

what would my family think? "No, I didn't hem your pants because I was too involved in the sunset." You see? It just wouldn't work. In our society, we're doers, not be-ers. Movers and shakers simply do not watch sunsets.

Also, there really are a lot of loose ends to tie up at that time of day. There's always somewhere to go or something to finish. Maybe some other day . . .

I didn't watch the sunset that day, or the next, or the next. But then came the early evening bike ride that changed things.

It was dusk, the split second between day and night, and lights were blinking on in all the houses I passed . . . all but one. I rode slowly by this lonely-looking house and remembered. Their lights hadn't been on for months. And they would not come on until someone bought the house. A car accident had seen to that—gone instantly—together. I remembered sitting with the old couple a year earlier. They had once lived in our present home and we enjoyed sharing stories. They had reared children, worked hard, and had their share of fun and heartaches in the same rooms we now occupied. Busy? Oh yes, they were busy. But after talking with them, I felt sure they had taken time for the calming influence of sunsets—and for the God behind them. And I could tell their lives had been enriched by moving over and making room for God in many small ways.

Now it was our turn. My family and I. We were walking just a few steps behind them in life experience—going through the same motions of living—headed for the same grave. And then eternity. No time for sunsets?

The next night I was there in a front-row seat waiting for the curtain to rise on the first act of sunset. The red glow of molten gold was a fitting benediction to another busy day—a perfect interlude for a talk with my almighty Friend. Devotions? That word was far too stilted to apply to this situation—this living, breathing interchange between the Creator and the created. I reveled in the shower of color which shouted the power and creative genius of the Originator. I watched the sun relax into a black silhouette of pines, dropping a golden curtain of night around the shoulders of the hills. God spoke to my spirit of his faithfulness as I meditated on the certainty of sunrise and sunset. He ministered to mind and heart as day tiptoed into night, and I found myself stretched out of a "cocoon of todayness" and into the vast reaches of God's eternity—the one prepared for me. I had found a healing block of solitude, a hermitage to talk to and listen to my God. It was a place to allow him to tie up the frayed edges of my thoughts and help me make sense out of the senseless.

Praise notes climbed out of my heart, tumbled over my lips. Serenity put eternal arms around me, and the words of an ancient lover of God came to mind:

It is not the dead who praise the LORD,
  those who go down to silence;
it is we who extol the LORD,
  both now and forevermore. [Ps. 115:17]

Let the name of the LORD be praised,
  both now and forevermore.
From the rising of the sun to the place where it sets,
  the name of the LORD is to be praised. [Ps. 113:2–3]

. . . and I knew I would meet him here again—often—before it was too late.

"Pothole" Christianity

Chuck Swindoll said it so well: "If you ask directions to your destination, and find out the road there is full of potholes, then every bump along the way is your assurance you're on the right road."

Make no mistake about it, "potholes" are promised. Look at Romans 5:3 and James 1 for starters. Talk about potholes! Curve balls! Detour signs! Red flags! And how come none of *these* promises are in our "promise" boxes or books of comfort?

Why potholes? Why, indeed. Because we are a part of the human race, and potholes are part of a package deal. Because we're earthbound until we're heaven bound. Because as long as we live we will wake up every day to a world diseased by the ungodly decisions of ungodly men. And sin always brings ragged sorrow.

Christians? Yes. Born-again ones? Yes. But you and I weren't snatched heavenward at the moment we believed. We still have our particular time slot to live out.

And because God does not force himself on man's will, we will often live with situations brought on by acts of men who refuse God.

So, what about potholes? What about Monday mornings, and broken hopes, and sickness, and the wretched tricks life likes to play? They are there. They won't go away. And we need to know how to handle them. At this point, God's Word turns question marks into exclamation points:

1. Potholes come with the territory, planet Earth.

   I have told you these things, so that in me you may have peace. In this world you will have trouble. But take heart! I have overcome the world. [John 16:33]

2. Christians aren't exempt. James addresses "brothers" in James 1:2.

3. Christians have special equipment to make the trip easier.

   His divine power has given us everything we need for life and godliness through our knowledge of him who called us by his own glory and goodness. [2 Peter 1:3]

4. Every pothole is happy assurance we're on the right road. This present world is the "right road" where the godly are assured of tribulations.

5. Every pothole is a chance to grow.

   For those God foreknew he also *predestined to be conformed to the likeness of his Son,* that he might be the firstborn among many brothers. [Rom. 8:29, italics added]

Romans 5 gives us lots of reasons not to stop too long or cry too hard at every pothole along the way:

100

1. We're clean in God's eyes (v. 1).
2. We have hope (v. 2).
3. We have peace with God (v. 2).
4. Potholes are concrete evidence that God is redesigning us to look like Jesus (v. 3).
5. God loved us. God loves us. God will love us (vv. 8–9).

Our circumstances don't change at the moment of salvation. We're shaken upside down and inside out by the grace of God and replanted back in the same garden: earth. But we're an altogether new piece of humanity. We now face in a new direction: heaven. We now have new goals: his. We now have the incredible and awesome gift of eternal life. We possess a new reason for living. We have hope. We have a heavenly Father in charge of our personal development and committed to our best interests. We are a part of a worldwide army of believers marching down the same road, headed for the same place. We are now under the umbrella of Almighty direction. We now have the very Spirit of God to help us pray, convict us of sin, comfort us, and give us power. We now have a guidebook that will never go out of print, written by God himself. And this guidebook has all the maps we'll ever need for the trip.

No, we're not exempt from trouble of all descriptions. We're empowered for it. Enabled to climb above it! Constrained by the very love of God to view trouble from his perspective! Invigorated by the Spirit of God he has placed within us! We have altogether new ability—a supernatural approach to potholes. We can look them in the face with tears streaming down our very human faces, and say, "I *know* that my redeemer liveth!" And, "No, in all these things we are more than conquerors through

101

him who loved us. For I am convinced that neither death nor life, neither angels nor demons, neither the present nor the future, nor any powers, neither height nor depth, nor anything else in all creation, will be able to separate us from the love of God that is in Christ Jesus our Lord" (Rom. 8:37). We have the unchangeable promise of the Almighty that all earth-times, for the Christian, will be woven together into a pleasing result as his wisdom fits the crooked places together (Rom. 8:28).

We are hallelujah people! Bought-with-a-price people! The eternity crowd, filled with truths that strangle despair and blot out hopelessness. We're "kids of the kingdom" . . . love slaves to a Master who is pledged never to leave us comfortless. We're travelers on a road that's only temporary . . . visitors with an eternal pass to heaven.

Potholes, for the Christian, are nothing more than an excuse to sing the Hallelujah Chorus one more time!

Closed Doors, Too

If you have ever, in your Christian journey, experienced "closed doors" . . . and beat your fists and cried and demanded the door be opened and seen no apparent change . . . if you have ever finally placed your destiny in the hands of God, trusting that this, too, is from him . . . you will enjoy this true experience that is retold in a way to protect the privacy of people on both sides of the door.

These are the words of him who is holy and true, who holds the key of David. What he opens, no one can shut, and what he shuts no one can open. [Rev. 3:7]

Once upon a life journey, there was a shut door I wanted to open . . . very badly. This door had been clearly shut for years, and I was tired of seeing it shut. I wasn't sure who had shut it or why. But in a starkly rebellious kind of way I wanted that door open.

Friends wondered why I didn't just turn the knob and open the door. After all, they had. I explained quite rationally that this particular door would open for some, but not for me. At least not so far. That's when I began to make plans to open the door. I saw no reason it should not swing wide at my touch when it seemed to open for everyone else. I would *make* it happen, if it was the last thing I did.

Some books led me to believe there are no shut doors for people who are persistent, work hard, and have a "go-for-it" mindset. Armed with that kind of artillery, how could any mission fail?

I found others who concurred with me. This served to. assure me I was on the right track. This door, we agreed, should be opened.

At this point, I began a private campaign to wrest the keys to this shut door from the two who had them: the Great Keeper of the Keys and my very earthly husband. Now the Great Keeper of the Keys and my husband thought alike about this matter. If the Keeper would have given the order, my husband would gladly have opened the door for me. But there was no such order. Without realizing it, I was arming for battle against the two most formidable forces of my life.

My husband listened when I talked about opening the door together. But he did not hand over the keys. I showed him facts and figures pointing out why doors like this *needed* to be opened. I did this not once, but many times. He shook his head no, and added, "Besides, I rather *like* the looks of the closed door." This served only to enrage me. I felt he must be blinded to all the wonders behind that closed door. But he was actually *enjoying* the door as it was! He was finding good points about the hinges and the size and the color of the door.

I had no use for this kind of attitude, and my urge to rebel became even stronger.

The door began to loom larger and larger in my imagination. It's not that there weren't a lot of open doors around—there were. But I wasn't seeing them. All I saw was one shut door.

Time went on, and I began to spend hours every day figuring how to open the closed door. One scheme would surface, then another. I tried them all . . . on both door-keepers. I wheedled and insisted with both my husband and the Great Keeper of the Keys. The door remained firmly shut.

Maybe I hadn't tried hard enough. And so began an all-out combat with my opposing forces, making the closed door the subject of every human conversation and every heavenward prayer. Surely the keepers would see that the door must have been shut by mistake in the first place. And surely they realized how pleasant and useful an open door would be for me—and for them. They didn't seem to.

At length, all strength spent, all resources depleted, all arguments exhausted, I began to seriously question the "rightness" of forcing the door open. Internal storms began to gather. I approached the keepers of the keys one last time, forcing the issue to a stand-off. It was time, I insisted, for the door to be opened. I got a re-sounding no for an answer, and storm clouds convened in my soul. One black Sunday passed. A second day began, as stormy as the one before. Would I really allow this closed door to affect my relations with the keepers this way? And if I did, wouldn't it mean continuous ripples of never-ending conflict? I answered questions as fast as they came—as honestly as I could. I read searching sections from the Guidebook and resistance began to crumble. I knew I had no choice—no good, happy choice but to raise the white flag. I needed to surrender to the deciding will of the keepers of the keys. Quiet. Unemotional. In-the-will surrender. No bells. No tears. It was over.

I wondered if that meant the door would now be closed permanently. Or would the keepers of the keys open it tomorrow? I didn't know. My stricken gaze moved slowly, painfully away from the closed door. My body was lead, my spirit stone. Acceptance and Resignation and Peace wrestled one last time with Pride and Stubbornness. The almighty Keeper slowly cultivated the dying embers of love for God in my heart. I was brought face to face with new truth. "This closed door is from him!" I had thought he was the Keeper only of open doors. I had insisted that this closed door must be opened because I wanted it open. He decided otherwise. He took me on a short journey where we met some recent acquaintances of mine: Pride, Self-pity, Resentment, and Lack of Faith. I didn't like any of them. And I didn't want them as guests any longer.

The battle was over. I had met the Lord of the Closed Doors, and learned that he closed this door out of his great God-heart of love, and because he had other directions in mind.

Full surrender—then peace. Now came the faith journey with the Keeper who promises to breathe into every desert a drop of dew big enough to reflect a rainbow—despite the clouds.

Dandelions of Affliction

*There is no place to go for a vacation from the abnormality of
the universe.*

—*Edith Schaeffer,* Affliction

Your body is talking to you more these days. Not
asking, *telling* you what to do. Not moving at your command. Not giving in to your whims and overindulgences
and wishes. Not making the grade. Not working
smoothly. Not predictable any more. It's in your way
more often than not, making you sit up and take notice.
Making you adjust activities—eliminate them. Making
demands you don't like at all.

It's never been this way. Always you made plans and
kept them. You told your body what to do and when,
and for how long. You were the master, your body the
servant. You ignored discomfort and went on. You fed
it well—it served you well. It doesn't make sense that
this should have happened. Your body was meant to bow

to your demands—always—wasn't it? And it has, most of the time. But now who's boss? You make plans and your body says "cancel." You take a new job and your body says "quit." You want to watch the late show just once, and your body shouts, "Not on your life!"

You thought there would be an end to it, but now you're not so sure. You keep waiting to get back in the mainstream of things, and you're beginning to wonder if this *is* the mainstream—for you—for now.

You know you ought to trust God now more than ever. But inside your naked spirit you're in a face-off with him. You're challenging his timing, his purpose, his love, his all-sufficient grace, his wisdom, and his promise that he works even bad experiences together "for the good" (Rom. 8:28). And quite frankly, you're angry at God for allowing your body to intrude on your plans. Can you possibly be any real good to the Lord like this? You're not any good to yourself half the time.

Then there are your friends, co-workers, and family. They were understanding at first. But this thing has dragged on. And sympathy wears thin quickly. People tire of *really* knowing how you are. Family members don't come right out and say it, but they want you to be right back where you were, because your body is in their way. Oh, they would never say it, but you can read it in their eyes when the work falls behind.

And you look so good! No one would ever know your body rules your nights and days. That's why you're expected to be in the mainstream—chin up and buckle down. So you try. And you fail. Your body shouts, "Listen to me!" and you ignore the call in your attempt to be a hero. Your pride pushes you on, and you blindly ignore the pleas of a body that can no longer do your bidding. The inevitable occurs, and you stumble to the doctor's office in worse condition than before.

What happens, then, when you can no longer function like you're used to functioning? How do you handle the demands that seem harmless but are really dangerous? Is there a way, as a believer, to learn to live with "dandelions" when your world has been full of "bouquets"?

I am eternally grateful to my heavenly Father that, from a knowledge of Scripture as well as the experience of others who have exhibited his grace, I can answer, "Yes, there is a way."

Bouquets of Grace

Dear believer, one healing response to bodies and minds that are afflicted is to live up to the name *believer*. *Believe* God when he says plainly that all things (both good and bad experiences) work together for good (Rom. 8:28). *Believe* because he is a God who is loving as well as all-powerful. Because he cannot lie.

Remember that in Jesus we have a high priest who *is* touched with the feeling of our infirmities. He understands! Just before his trial and crucifixion, Jesus was in dire agony of soul. He pleaded with God three times to remove the cup of suffering from him if there was any other way. Yet he said if there wasn't, "Thy will be done." He asked. He submitted. He left us a beautiful example of how to pray in the midst of affliction.

Give credit to God for knowing what he's doing, for he does (Matt. 28:18). And someday we will know.

Be honest when faith and trust drag in the dust. Cry out with the man in Scripture who said to Christ, "I do believe; help me overcome my unbelief!" (Mark 9:24).

Remind yourself that nothing can ever separate you from the love of God, or steal away your salvation (Rom. 8) or the promise of eternal life (John 3). And nothing will erase the fact that a perfect body is promised to us in eternity (1 Cor. 15). Soak yourself in truth. Saturate your thoughts with Scripture until self-pity is pushed aside and praise begins edging forward.

Accept the inevitable process of aging and change and sickness, and make appropriate adjustments in your lifestyle. The world doesn't rise or fall on whether *you* can perform. God's work has always gone on where it is his work.

Dear friend, desire to know Christ, and the power of his resurrection, and the fellowship of sharing in his sufferings (Phil. 3:10).

Try to loosen up and honestly laugh at yourself, because when you reach this plateau, acceptance will have become a healing reality, and you can go upward from there in your attitude.

Recognize that life is cyclical. Yesterday it was time for one pursuit, and today it may be time for another. Solomon realized this as he wrote Ecclesiastes 3. No endeavor or occupation need be set in cement for life. It is God's desire that we live each day as unto him regardless of how that is carried out: in suffering well or in active service. Who are we, the creature, to tell the creator he will be more glorified by one endeavor than another? Or to tell him that our good health will benefit him more than our sickness or infirmity?

The apostle Paul obviously thought he could "serve" God better if his physical ailment was removed. God said, in essence, no. "My grace will see you *through* this infirmity. I will enable you to become an overcomer in spite of it. My grace will be exhibited in you for centuries to come through your reaction to me in this suffering." And it has been.

Service for God is not limited to active work of some sort. The very finest kinds of service are sometimes exhibited by suffering Christians.

Suffering, of any sort, is not something to hide as though if we were good enough Christians we wouldn't be suffering (2 Cor. 11). In fact, hidden suffering may not as greatly glorify God, because his grace is also hidden. There are afflictions we tend to hide, such as alcoholism, depression, erring children. But discerning sharing with trusted people allows others to see God at his enabling best.

And we are not to pretend we are not suffering. Let's suffer honestly. Let's cry when we need to. To deny affliction is to say we are not a part of the human race. And it is to deny God the opportunity to demonstrate amazing grace. It is to shut ourselves off from the possibility of the greatest victories which others can share through prayer. It is to use up valuable energy denying, hiding, and skirting the fact of affliction. It is to pretend we are above and beyond anything but a sunshiny experience which is, of course, untrue.

The greatest of victories, the greatest of miracles, are perhaps those that are performed every day in the lives of those who are learning to walk through tragedy, sorrow, and depression, and who are experiencing God's grace in doing so.

These principles are fresh and are being fully tested in my own experience even as I write. I struggle now with new, postsurgical adjustments that are busily rearranging my "want tos" in a different order. I am not an onlooker. And I am just beginning to truly realize that God can glorify himself through a surrendered heart, no matter what circumstances (including a stubborn body) are whirling about.

God sometimes does take away affliction completely. He sometimes gives grace—overcoming grace—to endure the affliction rather than remove it. Where is the greater miracle? And isn't a spirit of "if it is not possible for this cup to be taken away . . . may your will be done" where it all begins? Read the account of Jesus' agony in the garden, and the events leading up to and beyond the cross to the resurrection. You'll find a God who is undeniably in the business of turning dandelions into bouquets of grace.

Bending Over, Standing Tall

The sunshine shimmered a halo of molten gold across the red-dirt country road south of Bristow, Oklahoma, as I walked with my mother. I was "back home" with Mom and Dad, and two weeks into recovery from radiation therapy. Cancer, surgery, and radiation had been a jolting interruption in my too-busy life. And a three-hour flight had temporarily rescued me from an anxious recuperation.

The Lord knew I needed spiritual reconditioning as well as physical refreshing. Upon arrival, my anxiety had peaked. Would I ever *really* be the same again? Would I ever shake this suffocating radiation fatigue and accompanying low spirits? Production had been a big part of my life. Make waves—get involved—leave footprints! But in February, the word *cancer* had called an abrupt halt to all production. I began crossing off my plans and writing in God's, asking, "What now, Lord?" His answer came in fits and starts.

114

The surgery itself had gone "swimmingly." God was more than enough. He was my strength and shield, and enabled my spirit in incredible ways. Three weeks after surgery, I was driving and enjoying social occasions with little difficulty. Life was moving right along. Then came the news I was a candidate for radiation therapy. "Precautionary measure," I was assured. I was disappointed, distressed, even angry. "Four and one-half weeks," the doctor smiled—"every day." He explained the side effects I could expect physically, and turned the lights out on my plans for another two months at least.

As the treatments progressed, their effect was cumulative. I was getting sick and tired by inches. Everyone kept saying how healthy I looked, but no one, including myself, knew what was going on inside. What was this innocent-looking machine doing to me? Every day it was robbing more energy and injuring my perfectly healthy organs in search of cancer cells to kill. "The healthy organs will recover," the doctor assured me. Every day my magnificent recovery, of which I was so proud, was taking a step backward. I was now learning to live with new problems. My expectations were getting holes shot through them. People were patient, but I wasn't. I was clearly losing this rat race to the swift and the healthy. Fatigue was doing a number on me and making big problems out of little ones.

In this state, I touched "home soil," and God began to go to work. He loved me through the Christ-like fragrance of a body of believers. He warmed me through the beauty of an opulent spring countryside. He healed me through the care of loving parents and a relaxed pace of living. He delighted me with bluebirds and honeysuckle, magnolia trees and roses in May, catalpa trees bent with their loads of white blossoms, mockingbirds, early morning walks, raindrops on roses, and fireflies—associations harking back to my childhood.

Over and over he repeated to my spirit, "Cease striving, and know that I am God." Was it a time for me to "become" rather than "do"? A time to be healed and served rather than a time to serve others? A time to recover instead of a time to work?

This morning, on our walk, I had come closer to the answer for "Why all this?" We heard a loud wail which Mother described as the shriek of a peacock. We walked another quarter of a mile and were welcomed into a fairy-tale yard by a relaxed couple named Joe and Lola Alarid. Three peacocks glowed in a brilliant fire of color under the morning sun. Our kindly hosts gave me an armload of the gorgeous feathers from this year's molt. Giant magnolia blossoms leaned down to kiss honeysuckle vines. Rosebushes, wet with dew, twined around a wagon wheel and cast showers of fragrance everywhere. Scores of happy martins chattered in and out of their newly-furnished birdhouses. And heaven seemed near at hand. Their happy home, a remodeled schoolhouse, nestled in sweet content amid this chorus of color and sound.

"Cease striving and know that I am God." Scripture was playing games in my head. God spoke again. "Stop fighting and resisting this experience. This, too, is from me. Listen to your body and don't be anxious. There is a time for everything."

"Even a time for recuperation that seems to never end?" I questioned. Bending down, I pressed my nose into the full, round fragrance of the roses. I noticed the metallic blue of a summer sky mirrored in the large, clear drops still on the petals. I gasped at the spectacular painting in miniature. It was a picture I never could have seen had I been walking straight and tall! Something clicked in my mind.

I clasped the sheaf of graceful feathers in one hand and the gift of purple wisteria in the other, and began to let go, to change, to grow toward an understanding—ultimately, to heal.

A True Story

This is the story not of one life but of many lives—of all lives that have known the overwhelming joy of fellowship with the living, loving Savior, but have watched that joy grow numb and pale and cold as death.

Sunrise

The sun rose like a shiny new penny and sent its cheering rays into the woman's life. She had just been born anew in Christ! It was dawn in her Christian life, and her faith was spring-green and healthy. She was consumed with the glowing passion of first love, and fired by the conviction that "no one could resist so great a salvation." What's more, she was convinced that no one would ever want to.

Her inner life was bright and alive, glowing with prisms of color that bathed her everyday landscape with reflections of heavenly hue. Jesus was her Savior and

Lord, and nothing—no one—could displace him in her affections. She drank deeply from the Word and shared everything with him in prayer.

No one had told her that a new Christian should study the Bible or pray or witness. But they didn't need to. It came naturally—supernaturally. She could do nothing else. Christianity was Christ! The psalmist expressed it for her:

As the deer pants for streams of water,
  so my soul pants for you, O God. [Ps. 42:1]

High Noon

The sun was a copper frying pan, reflecting the heat of noonday on a Christian life grown weary. An increasing exposure to the elements and a diminishing exposure to God's Word had drawn permanent lines, even furrows, on her forehead. She thirsted deeply; her tongue was parched. The water was available, but she hadn't stopped to drink lately. Didn't think she needed it. Dehydration had set in. An early death was certain unless she drank soon.

Cynicism had entered the heart of this careworn earthling. She opened the door to it, invited it inside to join Doubt. Faith and Trust were but memories. Her first love had dried and shriveled. The blossoms dropped early from her Christian life and the fountain of joy was plugged. She no longer told anyone of Christ—no longer shared the sunshine. She drew the blinds of belief and groped in the shadow of doubt. She had forgotten the blessings of prayer. Yet, Jesus waited. "Come to me, all you who are weary and burdened, and I will give you rest" (Matt. 11:28).

119

Sunset

A sickly sun drooped low on the horizon, hovered disconsolately for a moment, then disappeared. Only a dim, brooding glow gave evidence of a once-virile sunrise. A chill settled in, and the woman waited for darkness. She moved slowly now, and never without pain. She could no longer talk easily, and when she did, it was always of herself—not her Lord. Her hands shook too badly to write very often, and when she did, it was never of him. She wondered occasionally if he had forgotten her as she had forgotten him. The Bible said he would not, and somehow she knew this was true. But she could no longer read. She didn't even own a Bible anymore.

A smile came seldom. And when it did, it was the lopsided grin of the stroke victim. Sunset was here, night was closing in. Heaven was hers, but she had so little company to bring along with her. Sometimes she remembered the Christ of her first love. He had not changed. Why had she? How the joy had sung in her heart! But the melody had faded with time and neglect. A tear dropped on her wrinkled hand. Then it was too late to do more. Darkness had fallen.

> They will neither hunger nor thirst,
> nor will the desert heat or the sun beat upon them.
> He who has compassion on them will guide them
> and lead them beside springs of water. [Isa. 49:10]

Afterglow

This story could be written about you, about me. It's the story of anyone who has come to regard Bible study, prayer, and witnessing as mere Christian duties—as rou-

120

tine Christian chores—rather than royal privileges of a subject of almighty God himself, and who no longer enjoys fellowship with him.

Will it happen to you? to me? It certainly could. But only if we allow it. Only if we turn our backs on the wells of living water and choose to go live in the desert. Only if we reject the refreshment of God's daily presence and ignore the totality of his daily forgiveness. Only if we shut the doors of Sovereign love. Only if we walk away; only if we shut off the supply lines. Only if we choose to starve our souls, feeding on husks in an empty field while a banquet is available at the castle. Only if we give in to the paralyzing effects of lethargy. Then and only then will we watch joy die; watch our souls grow small and pinched and stone cold; watch them shrivel and curl up and prepare for burial; watch them die of starvation while living with a King. But only if we walk away.

It won't be God who changed toward us. It won't be God who moved away. That's not his way. It's yours, and it's mine.

The choice belongs to us.

The Artist and the Painting

The Lord got up this morning and began painting his usual masterpiece across the eastern edge of the sky. First came splashes of pink and lavender skillfully overlaid with brushstrokes of red-gold sun. Pearly fingers of sunlight danced gaily through greening branches and into the grass, laughing as they went. A choral kingdom of birds announced the birth of another new day in joyous response to the baton of an invisible director. The painting was coming into focus.

Blackbirds inched noiselessly through uncut grass in search of breakfast. Our pet bunnies nuzzled each other in hopes of the same. Mother cat yawned and stretched her newly-thinned body, prepared for another day of mothering. Sleepy workers moved routinely against the shimmering canvas of this new day, and hardly noticed.

I admired his other works of art as dawn unfolded gently into early morning: The smile he painted on my child's face—the trill of a mockingbird—the dark power of a surprise lightning flash cutting through charcoal skies—sparkling diamonds of dew on the roses. What would lie ahead for all of us before this day was over?

The painting, thus begun, was handed to me to complete, together with my own set of oils (2 Peter 1:3). I was not told what color to put here, what hue to emphasize there, or which shades to tone down. He simply gave me the best set of oils available and let me finish what he had begun. He stood by to encourage in case I spilled the paints or ruined the brushes (Matt. 28:20). He handed me new brushes when mine got stiff, and offered all the rich bounty of his eternal painting experience when I asked. Once I dropped the entire painting, but he didn't raise his voice—he just helped me pick up the pieces and begin again, and understand a little (James 1:5). Each new day he painted fresh new examples for my inspiration, but asked me to paint my own original—and gave me the confidence. He stood by me later, in the darkest hours of the early evening of a time when I couldn't see to paint, and others had left, and the pain set in. He held my hand steady when it began to waver and shake, and led me beside the still waters for extra refreshment (Ps. 23). Together we would complete this painting—he using my hands, I in his strength (Ps. 4:3). I had his word that the finished work would be part of a grand, final design he had in mind (Rom. 8:28). Someday I would understand the colors he handed me, and why he chose the canvases he did. And I would know why sometimes he gave me brushes that didn't seem to be any good. I would no longer ask when he was going to finish the mountain range or shade the rocks, or ask him to hurry up with his part of it. I would understand when he mixed the colors and sometimes used no color at all.

Some day the wondering would be finished, the painting complete. And I would know, because I would see the master Painter face to face (1 Cor. 13:12).